WORLD ENGLISH 1

Real People • Real Places • Real Language

Martin Milner

HEINLE
CENGAGE Learning™

Australia • Brazil • Japan • Korea • Mexico • Singapore • Spain • United Kingdom • United States

HEINLE
CENGAGE Learning™

World English 1
Real People • Real Places • Real Language
Martin Milner

Publisher: Jason Mann

Commissioning Editor: Carol Goodwright

Development Editor: Louisa Essenhigh

National Geographic Editorial Liaison: Leila Hishmeh

Technology Development Manager: Debie Mirtle

Director of Global Marketing: Ian Martin

Product Manager: Ruth McAleavey

Content Project Editor: Amy Smith

Senior Production Controller: Paul Herbert

Compositor: MPS Content Services

ISBN: 978-1-111-21646-7

Heinle
Cheriton House
North Way
Andover
Hampshire
SP10 5BE
United Kingdom

Cengage Learning is a leading provider of customized learning solutions with office locations around the globe, including Singapore, the United Kingdom, Australia, Mexico, Brazil, and Japan. Locate your local office at: **international.cengage.com/region**

Cengage Learning products are represented in Canada by Nelson Education, Ltd.

Visit Heinle online at **elt.heinle.com**

Visit our corporate website at **www.cengage.com**

Cover Image: Sergio Amiti/National Geographic Image Collection, Menara Gardens, Marrakech

Printed in Wales
2 3 4 5 6 7 8 9 10 - 15 14 13 12 11

CONTENTS

Unit	Unit Goals	Grammar	Vocabulary	Listening	Speaking and Pronunciation	Reading and Writing
UNIT 1 **People** page 2	• Meet people • Ask for and give personal information • Describe different occupations • Talk about people and their occupations	Review of present tense: *to be* *Be* + adjective (+ noun) Possessive nouns	Occupations Countries Nationalities Descriptive adjectives	Focused listening: Personal introductions	Asking for and giving personal information Contractions: *–'m, –'re, –'s*	"People from Around the World" Writing about a person and her occupation
UNIT 2 **Work, Rest, and Play** page 14	• Talk about a work day • Talk about free time • Describe a festival or a celebration • Compare different festivals	Review: Simple present tense Adverbs of frequency	Daily activities Party words	Focused listening: A radio celebrity interview	Talking about daily schedules and free time Verbs that end in *–s*	"Carnival: One Festival, Many Faces" Writing a descriptive paragraph
UNIT 3 **Going Places** page 26	• Identify possessions • Ask for and give personal travel information • Give travel advice • Share special travel tips with others	Possession Imperatives and *should* for advice	Travel preparations and stages Travel documents and money	General listening: Conversations at travel destinations	Giving personal information for travel forms Rising intonation in lists	"Smart Traveler: Expert Opinion" Writing travel tips
UNIT 4 **Food** page 38	• Talk about food • Order a meal • Talk about diets • Discuss unusual and favorite foods	Count and noncount nouns: *some* and *any* *How much, how many* with quantifiers: *lots of, a few, a little*	Food Diets	General and focused listening: In a restaurant	Role-play: purchasing food at a store Ordering from a menu Reduced forms: *Do you have . . .* and *Would you like . . .*	"Eating Seaweed" Writing a favorite recipe
UNIT 5 **Sports** page 50	• Talk about activities happening now • Compare every day and present time activities • Talk about favorite sports • Discuss adventure holidays	Present continuous tense Stative verbs	Doing sports Team sports Individual sports	General and focused listening: Every day activities vs. today's activities	Talking about what people are doing now Discussing favorite sports Reduced form: *What are you . . .*	"Climbing the Dragon's Spires" Writing an email
UNIT 6 **Destinations** page 62	• Talk about past vacation trips • Exchange information about vacations • Use *was/were* to describe a personal experience • Talk about a discovery from the past	Simple past tense Simple past tense: *to be*	Travel activities Emphatic adjectives	General listening: A vacation	Comparing vacations Describing personal experiences Sounds of *–ed* endings	"The City of Machu Picchu, the Cradle of the Inca Empire" Writing a postcard

Unit	Unit Goals	Grammar	Vocabulary	Listening	Speaking and Pronunciation	Reading and Writing
UNIT 7	**Communication** page 74 • Talk about personal communication • Give and write down contact details • Describe characteristics and qualities • Compare different types of communication	Verbs with direct and indirect objects Linking verbs	Communication Electronics The senses	Focused listening: A radio call-in program	Asking for contact information Describing sights, sounds and other sensations Endings –*ty* and –*teen*	"The Secret Language of Dolphins" Writing a text message
UNIT 8	**The Future** page 86 • Talk about plans • Discuss long and short term plans • Make weather predictions • Discuss the future	*Be going to* *Will* for predictions	Plans Weather conditions	General listening: A talk show	Talking about weekend plans Discussing the weather Reduced form of *going* to	"Future Energy" Writing statements about the future
UNIT 9	**Shopping for Clothes** page 98 • Make comparisons • Explain preferences • Talk about clothing materials • Understand and describe a process	Comparatives Superlatives	Clothing Descriptive adjectives Clothing materials	Focused listening: Shoe shopping	Talking about clothes Shopping—at the store and online Rising and falling intonation	"Silk—the Queen of Textiles" Writing about favorite clothes
UNIT 10	**Lifestyles** page 110 • Give advice on healthy habits • Suggest ways to improve bad habits • Ask about lifestyles • Evaluate your lifestyle	Modals—*could, ought to, should, must, have to* Questions with *how*	Healthy and unhealthy habits Compound adjectives	General listening: Personal lifestyles	Discussing healthy and unhealthy habits Giving advice for improving habits *Should, shouldn't*	"The Secrets of Long Life" Writing a paragraph about personal lifestyle
UNIT 11	**Achievements** page 122 • Talk about today's chores • Interview for a job • Talk about lifetime achievements • Discuss scientific achievements	Present perfect tense Present perfect tense vs. simple past tense	Chores Lifetime achievements	Listening for general understanding and specific details: A job interview	Interviewing for a job Catching up with a friend Reduced form of *have*	"Uncovering the Mysteries of the Universe" Writing an email to catch up
UNIT 12	**Consequences** page 134 • Talk about managing money • Make choices on how to spend your money • Talk about how our actions can have positive consequences • Discuss ways to prevent habitat destruction	Real conditionals (also called the First conditional)	Personal finances Animal habitats	Listening for specific details: At a travel agency	Making decisions about spending money Talking about important issues Sentence stress	"Habitat Destruction" Writing a letter to the editor

Get To Know

Brockworth, England
An unusual 200-year-old tradition from England. Chasing a ball of cheese down a very steep hill. *Cheese-Rolling Races*

Arizona, United States
Stress is part of life in the modern world. What can you do to control it? *The Science of Stress*

Orlando, Florida, United States
Join man's best friend as he looks for illegal food in American airports. *Beagle Brigade*

Hawaii
Find out more about the famous Hawaiian dance. *Hula*

Cuzco, Peru
Tourists come from all over the world to see the Lost City of the Incas. But is tourism destroying Machu Picchu? *Machu Picchu*

Your World!

Florence, Italy
Visit the last factory in Florence to make silk by hand.
Traditional Silk Making

Japan
The puffer fish: ugly, poisonous, and expensive. So, why do people like to eat it? *Dangerous Dinner*

Cheju Island, Korea
A group of women from Korea go diving every day to find seafood. Are they the last?
Korean Women Divers

North Africa
Learn how to use the sun's heat to cook your dinner.
Solar Cooking

Tanzania, Africa
The snows of Kilimanjaro are disappearing. Find out why. *Missing Snows of Kilimanjaro*

outh Africa
ow do African Bushmen ommunicate with onservationists? Is it vorking? *Wild Animal Trackers*

● = Sites of the video clips you will view in *World English 1*.

PEOPLE

1. Who are these people? Share your ideas with a partner.
   a. What are their names?
   b. How old are they?
   c. Where are they from?
   d. What do they do?
2. Are they like you?

UNIT GOALS

Meet people
Ask for and give personal information
Describe different occupations
Talk about people and their occupations

UNIT 1

A GOAL 1 MEET PEOPLE

Countries and Nationalities

Australia — Australian	Mexico — Mexican
Jordan — Jordanian	Peru — Peruvian
Bahrain — Bahraini	Thailand — Thai
France — French	Ireland — Irish

Occupations

chef	teacher	police officer
engineer	doctor	travel agent
pilot	photographer	

Engage!

Which occupations do you think are the most difficult?

Real Language

We say *what does she/he do* to ask about a person's occupation or job.

Vocabulary

A. Fill in the blanks. Use words from the boxes.

1. This is Carlos. He's a ___chef___ from ___Mexico___.
2. This is Maria. She's a ________ from ________.
3. This is Frank. He's a ________ from ________.
4. This is Nicolas. He's a ________ from ________.
5. This is Mohamed. He's an ________ from ________.
6. This is Fatima. She's a ________ from ________.
7. This is Sutanee. She's a ________ from ________.
8. This is David. He's an ________ from ________.

B. Work with a partner. Talk about the people in the pictures.

Carlos is from Mexico.

Oh, he's Mexican. What does he do?

He's a chef.

Grammar: *Be*

Statements with *be*

Subject pronoun	*be*	Negative	
I	**am**		
You/We/They	**are**	not	a chef.
He/She/It	**is**		

***Yes/no* questions**

Be	Pronoun		Short answers
Are	you/they	Mexican?	Yes, I am. No, I'm not.
Is	he/she/it		Yes, they are. No, he isn't.

Subject pronoun + *be*		*Be* contractions	
I am		**I'm**	
You/We/They are	Thai.	**You're** **We're** **They're**	Thai.
He/She/It is		**He's** **She's** **It's**	

A. Match the questions and the answers.

1. Are you a doctor? ____
2. Is she Korean? ____
3. Is Ben British? ____
4. Are you American? ____
5. Are Mario and Teresa students? ____

a. Yes, he is.
b. No, she isn't. She's Japanese.
c. Yes, they are. They come from Argentina.
d. No, I'm not. I'm a nurse.
e. No, I'm not. I'm Canadian.

B. Fill in the blanks with a pronoun and the correct form of the verb *be*.

1. ____________ from Japan. I'm from Thailand.
2. ____________ from Indonesia? Yes, I am.
3. Where ____________ from? They're from China.
4. ____________ an architect. He's a doctor.
5. ____________ from Canada? No, we're from the United States.

Conversation

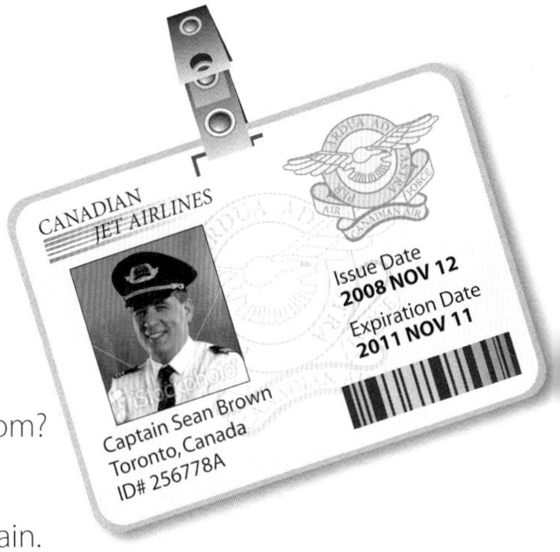

Track 1-2

A. Listen to the conversation. Where is Sean from?

Sean: So, Claudia, where are you from?
Claudia: I'm from Chile.
Sean: So, you're Chilean, eh. Sounds cool. Are you from Santiago?
Claudia: Yes, I am. And you, Sean? Where are you from?
Sean: I'm Canadian.
Claudia: Wow! Canada. I'd love to go to Canada. Which city are you from?
Sean: I'm from Toronto.

B. Practice the conversation with a partner. Switch roles and practice it again.

Goal 1 Meet people

Work with a partner. Create new personal IDs. Use the conversation above to meet each other.

Listening

A. Look at the pictures. Talk to a partner. Guess the missing information.

B. Listen to the TV game show. Fill in the blanks with the correct information.

Track 1-3

1. **Name:** Kyoko Hashimoro
   Nationality: ______________________
   City: Tokyo
   Country: Japan
   Occupation: ______________________

2. **Name:** Luis Gomez
   Nationality: ______________________
   City: Bogota
   Country: ______________________
   Occupation: ______________________

3. **Name:** Jim Waters
   Nationality: ______________________
   City: Coldstone
   Country: ______________________
   Occupation: Farmer

4. **Name:** Bianca da Silva
   Nationality: ______________________
   City: Rio de Janeiro
   Country: ______________________
   Occupation: Musician

C. Listen again. Check your answers.

Track 1-3

Pronunciation: Contractions of *be*

Track 1-4

A. Listen and repeat.

1. I am — I'm
2. you are — you're
3. he is — he's
4. she is — she's
5. it is — it's

Track 1-5

B. Listen. Circle the verb or contraction you hear. Then listen again and repeat.

1. I am/I'm a teacher.
2. He is/he's an engineer.
3. She is/she's not a nurse.
4. They are/they're interesting.
5. You are/you're welcome.

Communication

Student A chooses a card. **Student B** guesses the card by asking questions.

B: Are you 28 years old? — **A:** No, I'm not.
B: Are you a doctor? — **A:** Yes, I am.
B: Are you Argentinean? — **A:** No, I'm not.
B: Is your name Helen? — **A:** Yes, it is.

Name: Andrew
Nationality: American
Age: 28
Job: Teacher

Name: Pablo
Nationality: Argentinean
Age: 28
Job: Doctor

Name: Mi Hi
Nationality: Korean
Age: 23
Job: Architect

Name: Ana
Nationality: Argentinean
Age: 23
Job: Teacher

Name: Kwan
Nationality: Korean
Age: 30
Job: Architect

Name: Helen
Nationality: American
Age: 30
Job: Doctor

Goal 2 Ask for and give personal information

Interview some of your classmates. Ask their name, their age, and the job they do or want to do.

Language Expansion: Descriptive adjectives

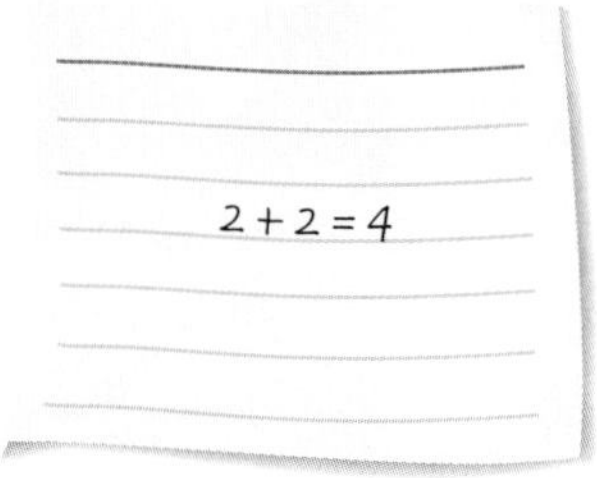

▲ easy

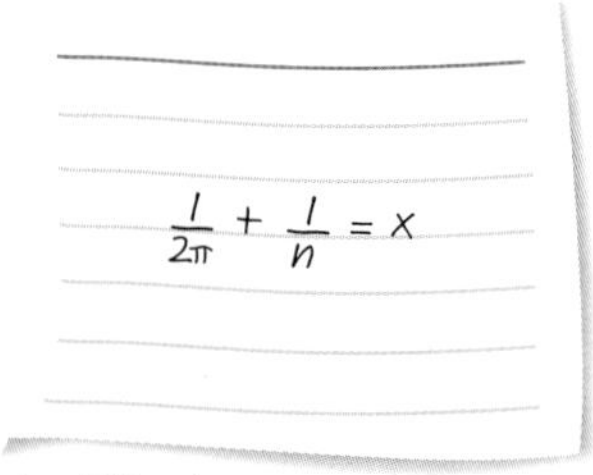

▲ difficult

▲ happy

▲ unhappy

▲ boring

▲ interesting

▲ rich

▲ poor

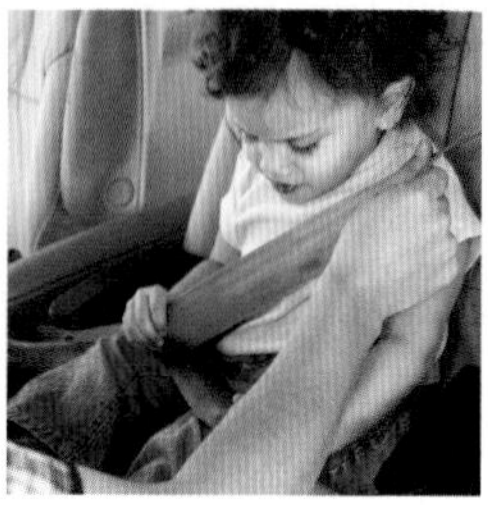

▲ safe

▲ dangerous

A. Write the words in the correct column.

Good	Bad
happy	unhappy

Word Focus

salary = money earned by the work you do

B. Fill in the blanks with adjectives.

Mrs. Green is ____________, but she is not happy. Why? Her husband's job is ____________. He is a helicopter pilot.

Mr. Green says, "I like my job. It is an ____________ job and the **salary** is ____________. It's not dangerous. In fact, it's very ____________." But Mrs. Green is still ____________.

Grammar: *Be* + adjective (+ noun)

Subject	*Be*	Adjective
My friend	is	rich.
His job	is	dangerous.
I	am	not happy.
My brother's job	is	interesting.

Subject	*Be*	Article	Adjective	Noun
It	is	an	easy	job.
Your friend	is	an	interesting	person.
It	is	a	difficult	life.

A. Circle the correct word or phrase in the parentheses.

1. My father's job is (interesting/an interesting). He is a newspaper photographer. It's not (easy/ an easy) job but he enjoys it.
2. I am a teacher. The salary isn't very (good/a good). I'm not (rich/a rich).
3. John is an engineer. It's (difficult/a difficult) job but it's (interesting/an interesting) job.

Possessive Adjectives

This is **my** friend.
Is that **your** brother?
His/her friend comes from Uruguay.
Their parents are nice people.

*Possessive nouns are formed with an apostrophe (') + -s.
*Laura**'s** friend is from London.*

B. Unscramble the words to write sentences.

1. job friend's is My dangerous.
   ____
2. is person. interesting Kim's friend an
   ____
3. your brother happy? Is
   ____
4. rich is not a My father man.
   ____
5. Chile. friend John's from is
   ____

Conversation

A. Listen to the conversation. What does Graham do?

Track 1-6

Graham: What do you do, Elsa?
Elsa: I'm an engineer.
Graham: An engineer! That's interesting.
Elsa: Yes, but it's difficult work. And you, Graham? What do you do?
Graham: I'm a policeman.
Elsa: A policeman! Is it dangerous?
Graham: No, in fact, sometimes it's boring.

B. Practice the conversation with a partner. Switch roles and practice it again.

Goal 3 Describe different occupations

Work with a partner. Take turns. Choose an occupation and say two things about it.

D GOAL 4 TALK ABOUT PEOPLE AND THEIR OCCUPATIONS

Reading

A. Look at the pictures. What do these people do?

B. Circle **T** for *true* and **F** for *false*.

1. Peter is a pilot. T F
2. Rimii Sen is Indian. T F
3. Alan Kirby's job is boring. T F
4. Angutikavsak's life is not easy. T F
5. Tanya is a teacher. T F

C. Answer the questions.

1. Where is Tanya from? ______________________
2. Who is Shep? ______________________
3. Why does Alan like his job? ______________________
4. What does Angutikavsak do? ______________________
5. What does Rimii say about her job? ______________________

People from Around the World

Angutikavsak is from Greenland, and he is a hunter. All his friends are hunters too.

"It is a difficult life here. In winter, it is very cold. We are not rich, but we are happy." he says.

Peter Elworthy is from New Zealand. He is not a pilot; he is a farmer! His farm is very big, so he uses an airplane. Peter's dog, Shep, is also in the plane.
"Is Shep frightened in the plane?" I ask.
"No, he's happy. He loves flying."

Rimii Sen is a TV producer. She is Indian, and she is from Mumbai. 'People think a TV producer's life is exciting, but it is difficult work. However, the salary is good!"

Tanya Rogers is from Boulder, Colorado, in the United States. She is a student, and she is also a musician. "I love my music, but it's very cold here in winter."

This is Alan Kirby, and he is a policeman. He's from New York. "A policeman's work is not boring, and I like helping people."

Writing

Write about André and his occupation.

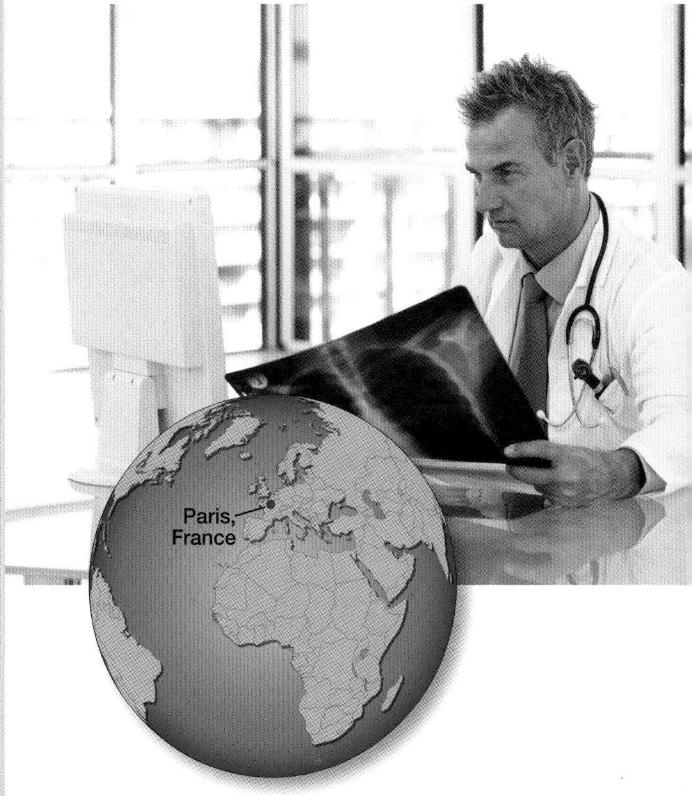

____

____

____

____

____

✓ Goal 4 **Talk about people and their occupations**

Work with a partner. Talk about a friend or family member and their occupation.

E VIDEO JOURNAL *THE LAST OF THE WOMAN DIVERS*

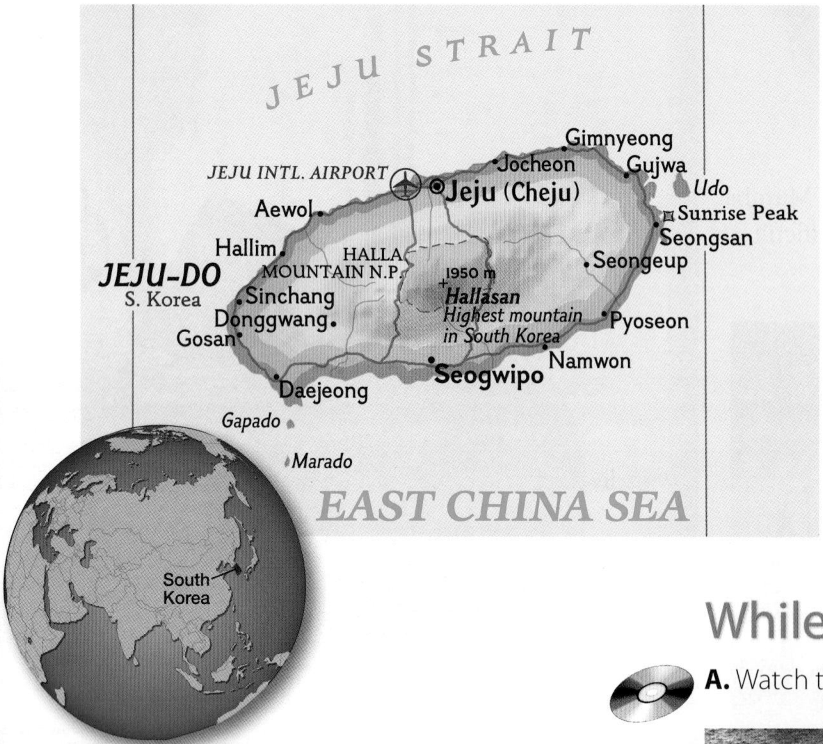

Before You Watch

Fill in the blanks. Use the words in the box.

tour guide	**divers**	**seafood**

In Korea, there is a group of women ______________________. They go to the sea every day to catch ______________________, like octopus and shellfish. Some of the women are not divers. One of them works with tourists. She is a ______________________.

While You Watch

A. Watch the video and fill in the blanks.

Name: Sunny Hong

Country: Korea

Nationality: ______________________

Occupation: ______________________

Age: 28

Name: Ms. Hong

Country: ______________________

Nationality: Korean

Occupation: ______________________

Age: ______________________

B. Watch again. Circle **T** for *true* and **F** for *false*.

1. Diving is difficult and dangerous. T F
2. The water is cold. T F
3. The divers can stay underwater for 10 minutes. T F
4. Sunny Hong is a diver. T F
5. The women sell the seafood. T F

After You Watch

Sunny Hong speaks English. She is a tour guide. She is not a diver. She says, "I am lucky." How can speaking English help *you*?

Communication

1. Write jobs in the chart.

Jobs women do well	Jobs men do well

2. Work with a partner. Compare your lists. Are they the same? Do you agree with your partner?

WORK, REST,

1. Which word or phrase describes each photo?
   a. work day
   b. weekend
   c. festival
   d. celebration

2. Where do you want to be? Why?

UNIT GOALS

Talk about a work day
Talk about free time
Describe a special celebration or festival
Compare different festivals

AND PLAY UNIT 2

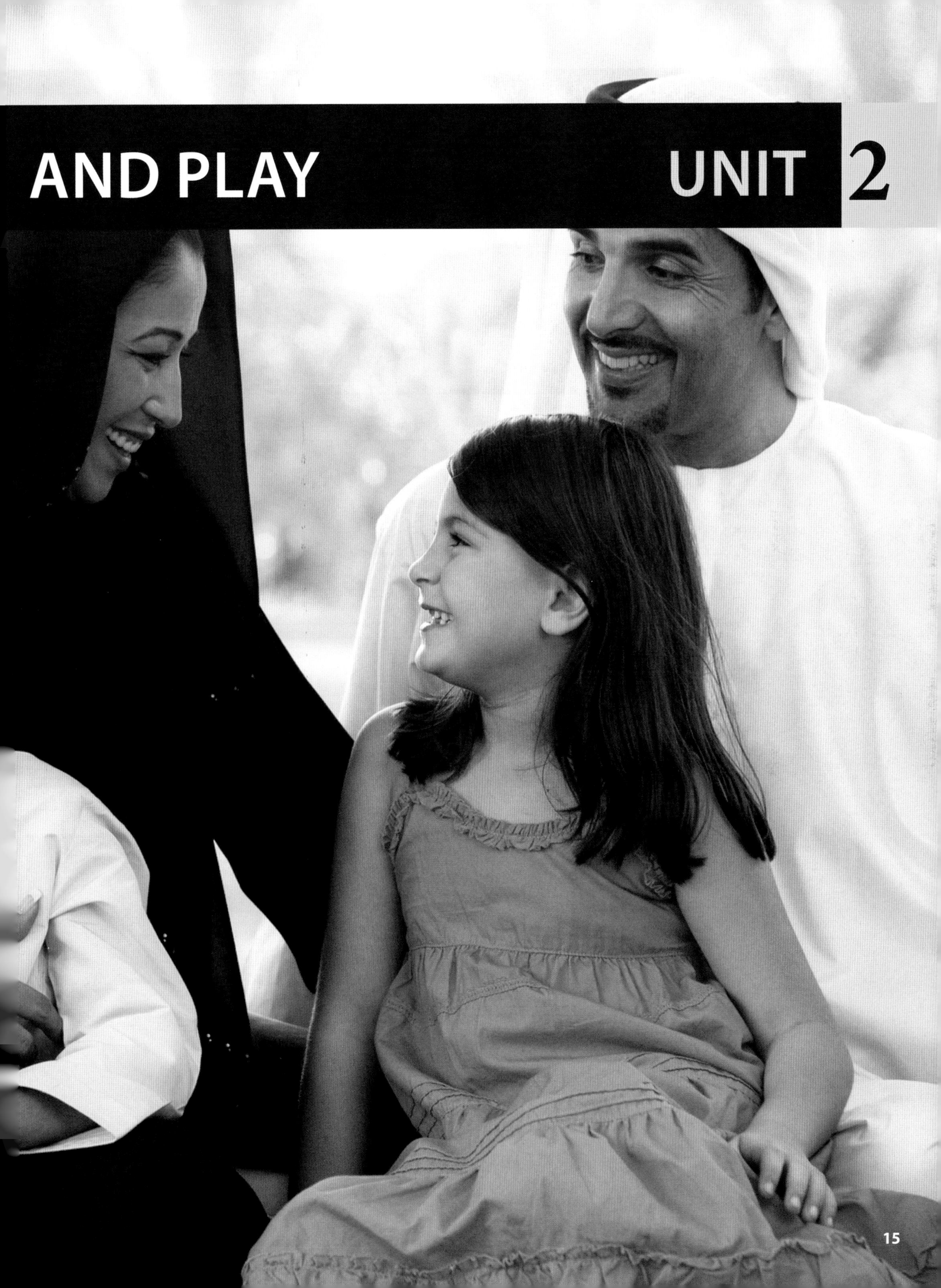

Vocabulary

A. Label the pictures. Use phrases from the box.

read the newspaper
get up
eat breakfast
go to bed
take a shower
catch the bus
go to the park
take a nap
watch TV
visit friends
start work
eat out

a. ____________________

b. ____________________

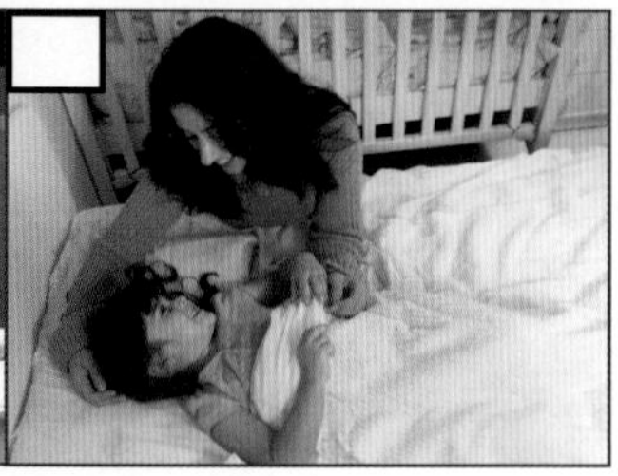

c. ____________________

d. ____________________

e. ____________________

f. ____________________

g. ____________________

h. ____________________

i. ____________________

j. ____________________

k. ____________________

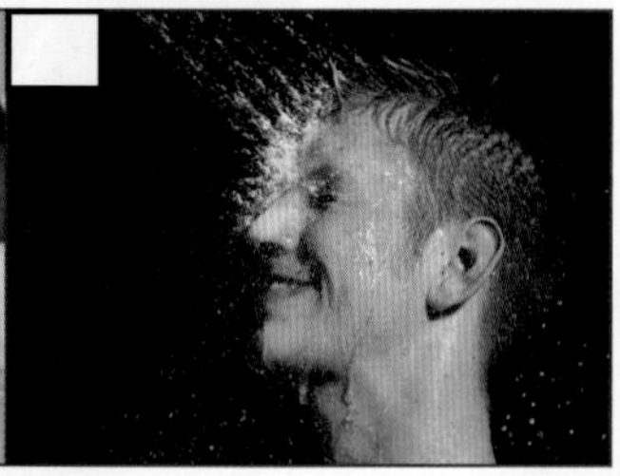

l. ____________________

First I get up, **then** I take a shower, **next** I get dressed . . .

B. Circle the activities in exercise **A** that you do every day.

C. In what order do you do these activities? Number the pictures.

D. Describe your daily routine to a partner. Use *first*, *next*, *then*, *finally*.

Grammar: Simple present tense

Simple present tense		
Statements	**Negative**	
I/you **start** work at eight o'clock. Alison **catches** the bus at five-thirty. We/They **go** to the park every Saturday.	I/you **don't start** work at eight o´clock. Alison **doesn't catch** the bus at five-thirty. We/they **don't go** to the park every Saturday.	
***Yes/ no* questions**	**Short answers**	
Do you **start** work at eight o'clock? **Does** Alison **catch** the bus at five-thirty? **Do** we/they **go** to the park every Saturday?	Yes, I do. Yes, she does. Yes, we/they do.	No, I don't. No, she doesn't. No, we/they don't.
*We use the simple present tense to talk about habits and things that are always true.		

Complete the exchanges (questions and answers) with information from the date book.

1. **Q:** What time do you __________?
   A: I get up __________ seven o'clock.
2. **Q:** __________ you watch TV in the morning?
   A: No, I __________ watch TV in the morning.
3. **Q:** What time __________ start work?
   A: He starts work __________.
4. **Q:** Do they __________ at ten o'clock?
   A: No, they go to bed __________.

Prepositions of time		
on	**in**	**at**
on Saturday(s) on the 4th of July on National Day	in the morning in the afternoon in the evening	at eight o'clock at night

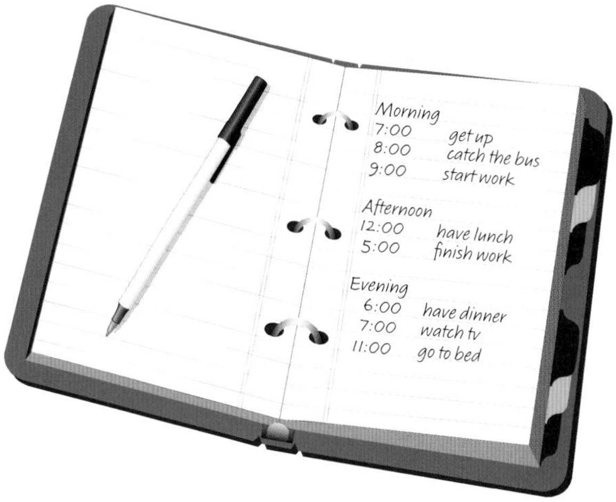

Conversation

A. Listen to the conversation. Does Mia work on Saturday?

Track 1-7

Chris: So, Mia, you're a secretary.
Mia: That's right.
Chris: What time do you start work?
Mia: At nine o'clock.
Chris: Do you work on Saturday?
Mia: Yes, I do, but we finish work at twelve o'clock on Saturdays.
Chris: What do you do in the evenings?
Mia: I watch TV or read the newspaper.

B. Practice the conversation with a partner. Switch roles and practice it again.

Goal 1 Talk about a work day

Talk with your partner about your work day.

Listening

Track 1-8

A. Listen to the interview with Bob Hardy. What is Bob talking about? Circle the correct answer.

a. his daily routine
b. his free time
c. his work

Track 1-8

B. Listen again. Circle the correct answer.

1. On Sundays, Bob gets up at ____.
   a. eight o'clock
   b. nine o'clock
   c. ten o'clock
2. In the morning he ____.
   a. reads the newspaper
   b. visits friends
   c. goes to the park
3. What does he do at one o'clock?
   a. He has lunch.
   b. He takes a nap.
   c. He visits friends.
4. What does he do in the evening?
   a. He watches TV.
   b. He goes out for a meal.
   c. He reads.

Pronunciation: Verbs that end in *-s*

Track 1-9

A. Listen and check (✓) the correct column.

	Ends with /s/	Ends with /z/	Ends with /iz/
starts			
comes			
catches			
watches			
gets			
eats			
goes			

Track 1-9

B. Listen again. Repeat the words.

Communication

Work with a partner. Fill in the date book with your information. Then fill in your partner's information. Ask questions like:

> What do you do in the evening?

> What time do you have breakfast?

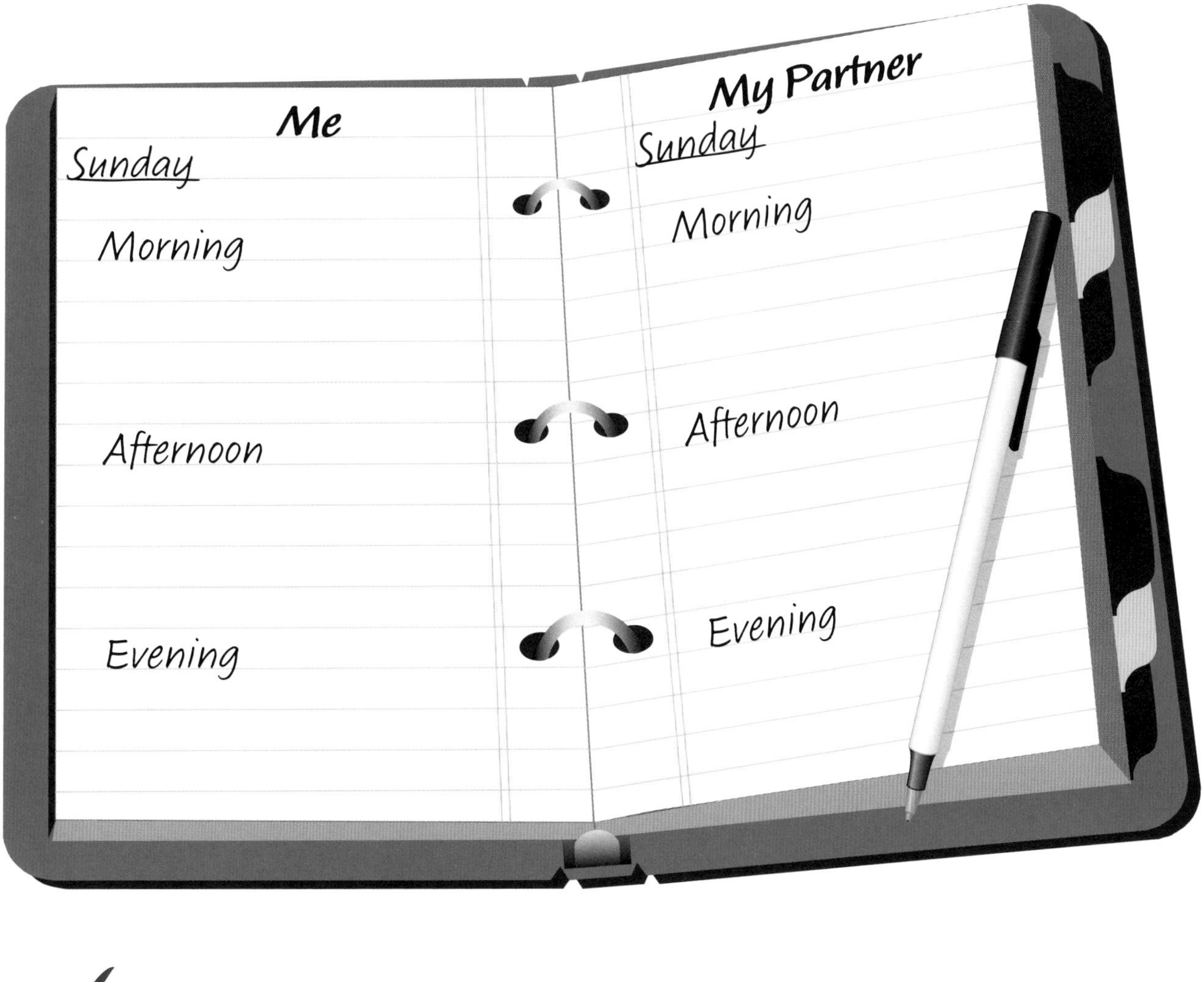

Goal 2 Talk about free time

Talk with a partner about your free time.

▲ In the United States, Americans always end their Independence Day celebrations with **fireworks**.

▼ In Venice, people wear **costumes** and cover their faces with **masks** to celebrate Carnival.

Language Expansion: Party words

A. Read the text. Pay attention to the words in **blue**.

All around the world, people need to **celebrate**. During the week we work, on weekends we rest, but we also need to have fun. Festivals are special celebrations. During festivals, people wear different clothes, eat special food, and give **presents** to friends and family.

◀ People in India enjoy Diwali, the Festival of Lights. They **decorate** streets and houses with lights of many colors.

◀ In July every year, Spaniards and tourists run with the bulls in Pamplona. It is very dangerous, but they say it's **fun**.

B. Complete the sentences with the words in **blue** from exercise **A**.

1. We watch the ____________________ on New Year's.
2. I love parties. You can see all your friends. It's ____________________!
3. At Halloween, children wear ____________________ and ____________________ to cover their faces.
4. We ____________________ New Year on the 1st January.
5. At New Year in Turkey, they ____________________ trees with colored lights and put ____________________ under it for friends and family.

Grammar: Adverbs of frequency

0% ____ **100%**

never **sometimes** **often** **always**

Word order

Subject	Adverb of frequency	Verb	
We	always	give	presents on New Year's Day.
We	never	decorate	the streets at Christmas.
Subject	***Be***	**Adverb of frequency**	
New Year's Eve	is	always	in December.
Carnival	is	usually	in February or March.

*We use adverbs of frequency to say how often we do something.
*Adverbs of frequency come **before** the verb.
*Adverbs of frequency come **after** *be*.

A. Unscramble the words to make sentences. Write the sentences.

1. always We have a on New Year's Day turkey.
____
2. New Year. never I send cards at
____
3. sometimes on visit our We neighbors New Year's.
____
4. Alan his forgets wife's sometimes birthday.
____
5. go They the park often to on the weekend.
____

B. Take turns. Tell a partner what sentences in exercise **A** are true for you.

Conversation

A. Listen to the conversation. Does Carol have a family meal on New Year's?

Track 1-10

Neil: What do you do on New Year's Day?
Carol: Well, we sometimes go downtown. They have fireworks. It's really pretty. Other people invite friends to their house and they have a party.
Neil: Do you give presents to your friends and family?
Carol: No, we never give presents on New Year's.
Neil: Do you have a meal with your family?
Carol: No, we do that on Christmas. On New Year's we just party!

Real Language

We say *we party* when we have fun with friends.

B. Practice the conversation with a partner. Switch roles and practice it again.

Goal 3 **Describe a special celebration or festival**

Talk with a partner about your favorite celebration or festival.

Reading

A. Look at the photos. Guess the country.

▲ The costumes often take a year to make and cost thousands of dollars.

► Schools take part in the Carnival parade.

B. Circle **T** for *true* or **F** for *false*.

1. People often wear costumes for Carnival. T F
2. The writer comes from Trinidad. T F
3. In New Orleans, people dance in the street at Carnival. T F
4. Carnival is in May. T F
5. There are Samba schools in Venice. T F

Trinidad and Tabago

Carnival: One Festival, Many Faces

A girl throws yellow paint in my face. I'm not angry. I laugh and I throw paint at her. This is fun! This is Carnival—Trinidad style.

Carnival is a festival that takes place every year. The date changes but it is usually in February or March.

▲ More than 300,000 tourists come to New Orleans for Carnival. And they spend half a billion dollars!

Around the world people celebrate Carnival in different ways. In Rio de Janeiro, schools spend a year making fantastic costumes for the Carnival parade. In Venice, they wear beautiful masks. In some parts of Germany, for one day the women take control of the town and cut off men's **ties**. Here in Trinidad, people party!

It is two o'clock in the morning on *Dirty Monday* and we are having a street party. People get dressed in old clothes and throw mud and paint at each other. But tomorrow the serious celebrations begin. People spend the whole year making costumes for Carnival. Tomorrow is their big day. There is a competition for the best costumes. The winners get money and a car. It's serious business.

So, why don't *you* come to Trinidad to celebrate Carnival?

Word Focus

tie = a long piece of cloth worn around the neck; usually worn by men.

Writing

Write about a festival in your country. Answer these questions.

a. What is the name of the festival?
b. When do you celebrate the festival?
c. Why do you celebrate this festival?
d. What do you do?

Songkran is a very important festival in Thailand. It is the Thai New Year and we celebrate it from the 13th to the 15th of April.

We celebrate it to say goodbye to the old year and to welcome the new year.

Traditionally, at Songkran we visit old people to pay respect. And many people clean their houses. But the best part of Songkran is when we throw water at other people in the street. We even throw water at strangers, but they do not get angry. It's just good fun.

Goal 4 **Compare different festivals**

Share your writing with a partner. Tell your partner how your festival is different from Carnival.

E VIDEO JOURNAL *HULA*

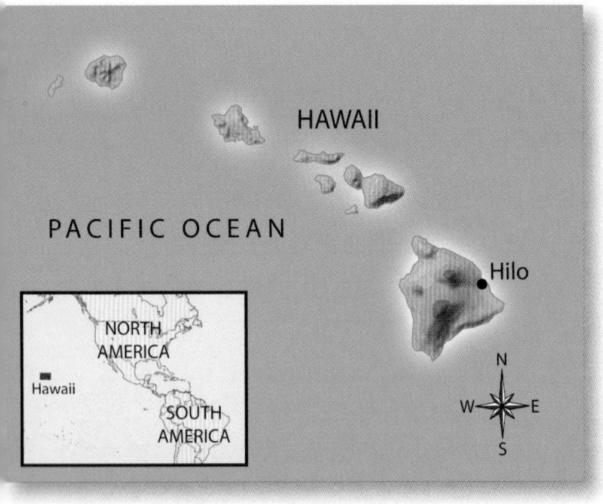

Before You Watch

A. Where are these dances from?

B. Study the words and definitions. Use the words in the box to complete the sentences.

legends = stories about the past
waves= movement on water
missionary = a person who brings a new religion to a country
surprised = when you don't expect something
judge = a person who decides which person is the winner

1. Juan and Maria are together again. I'm ________________!
2. Old people tell ________________ to young children.
3. My uncle is a ________________ in Africa.
4. It is dangerous to swim here. The ________________ are very big.
5. The ________________ is wrong! I am the winner.

While You Watch

A. Watch the video. Number the sentences in the correct order.

___ But some Hawaiian people dance the hula in secret.
___ The hula starts 300 years ago.
___ The missionaries tell the queen of Hawaii to stop the dance.
___ The hula dancers take part in a festival every year.
___ Today there are special schools where people learn the hula.

B. Watch the video again. Circle the correct answer.

1. The hula is ___ years old.
   a. 300
   b. 3000
2. The girls in the legend copy the ___.
   a. waves
   b. trees
3. The missionaries were ___.
   a. surprised
   b. interested
4. The dancers have to practice for many ___ before they can perform.
   a. days
   b. hours
5. The judges look at the dancers' ___.
   a. hair
   b. costumes

After You Watch

Talk with a partner. What traditional dances do you have in your country? What is your favorite dance?

Communication

Describe the pictures to a partner. Talk about the following.

a. Where are the dancers from?
b. Are the people happy?
c. Which dance do you like most? Why?

GOING PLACES

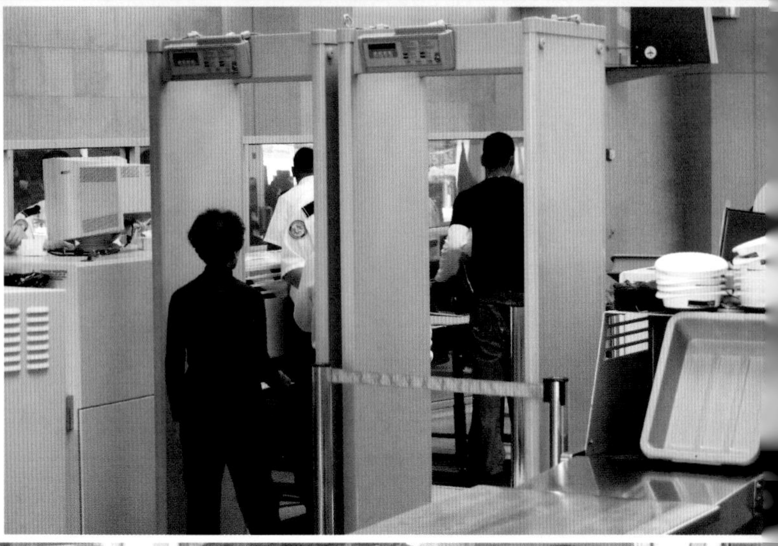

1. Which word best describes each picture?
   a. boarding gate
   b. baggage carousel
   c. check-in desk
   d. security

2. What do you do at these places?

UNIT GOALS

Identify possessions
Ask for and give personal travel information
Give travel advice
Share special travel tips with others

UNIT 3

13
QATAR AIRWAYS
QR154
12:50
Gate
2
Doha International Airport
Doha International Airport

A GOAL 1 IDENTIFY POSSESSIONS

Vocabulary

A. In what order do you do these things? Number the pictures.

▲take a taxi

▲pack your bags

▲go through customs

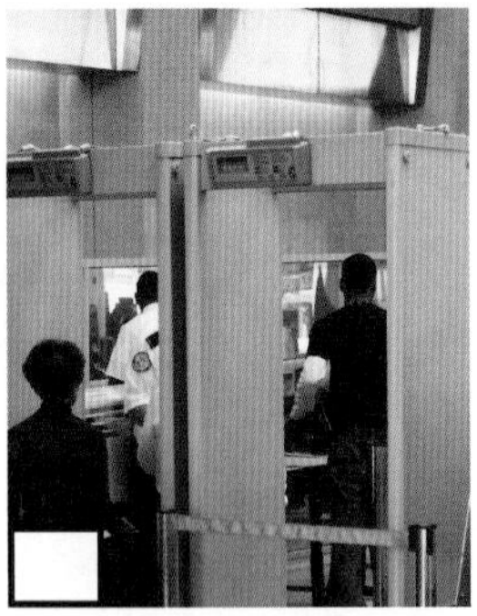

▲go through security

▲buy your ticket

▲board the airplane

▲claim your baggage

▲go through immigration

▲check in

▲buy duty free goods

B. Complete the sentences. Use a phrase from exercise **A**.

1. After you ______________________, you can leave the airport.
2. Do I have to take off my shoes when I ______________________?
3. At the airport, the first thing you do is ______________________.
4. Many people ______________________ like perfume and chocolates at the airport.
5. When you ______________________ you can only take a small bag.
6. Make sure you don't take the wrong bag when you ______________________ at the carousel.

Grammar: Possession

Possessive adjective	Possessive pronoun	*Belong to*	
my	mine	It **belongs to**	me.
your	yours		you.
his	his		him.
her	hers		her.
our	ours		us.
their	theirs		them.

Real Language

To ask about possession we can say *Whose ____ is this?*

A. Complete the conversations. Use a word or phrase for possession.

A: Excuse me. Is this ______________________ bag, Karen?
B: No, it's not ______________________.
A: Is this Anna 's bag?
B: No, ______________________ is green.
A: ______________________ ticket is this?
B: I think it ______________________ Shawn.

B. Answer the questions using *belong to* and a possessive pronoun.

1. Whose passport is this? (Ali) It belongs to Ali. It's his.
2. Whose keys are these? (my keys) ______________________
3. Whose camera is this? (my sister's) ______________________
4. Whose bags are these? (John and Lucy's) ______________________
5. Whose tickets are these? (Logan's and mine) ______________________

Conversation

A. Listen to the conversation. Who does the bag belong to?

Track 1-11

Anna: Whose bag is this?
Bill: It's not mine.
Anna: Maybe it's Jim's. Is this your bag, Jim?
Jim: No, mine is black.
Anna: Well, whose is it?
Bill: Maybe it belongs to this woman. Excuse me, does this bag belong to you?
Woman: Yes, it's mine. Thank you so much.

B. Practice the conversation in a group of four students. Switch roles and practice it again.

Goal 1 Identify possessions

Work with a partner. Use the conversation for ideas to ask about different possessions.

Listening

Track 1-12

A. Listen to the conversations. Where do the conversations take place?

Conversation 1 ______________________________

Conversation 2 ______________________________

Conversation 3 ______________________________

▲ hotel reception

Track 1-12

B. Listen again. Circle **T** for *true* and **F** for *false.*

Conversation 1

1. The man books a window seat. T F
2. The man has two bags. T F

Conversation 2

1. This is the woman's first visit to the United States. T F
2. The woman is staying in the United States for three weeks. T F

Conversation 3

1. The man is staying at the hotel for one night. T F
2. The man has one bag. T F

▲ immigration

Track 1-12

C. In which conversation did you hear these questions? Listen again and check your answers.

1. Is this your first time in the United States? 2
2. Can I see your U.S. visa, please? ___
3. Where are you staying? ___
4. Is this your bag? ___
5. Can I see your passport, please? ___
6. Can I see your ticket and passport, please? ___
7. What is the purpose of your visit? ___
8. Window or aisle seat? ___

▲ check-in counter

Pronunciation: Rising intonation on lists

Track 1-13

A. Listen and repeat the sentences.

1. I'm going to London ↗, Paris ↗, Rome ↗, and Madrid ↘.
2. I've got my camera ↗, cell phone ↗, laptop ↗, and Palm™ ↘.
3. You can take a taxi ↗, the shuttle bus ↗, or a rental car ↘.

B. Practice these sentences with a partner.

1. We want to travel by bus, train, plane, and taxi.
2. I need to pack a sweater, a jacket, a scarf, and a warm hat.
3. Let's visit Argentina, Brazil, Chile, and Peru.
4. When I get to the hotel, I need to check in, take a shower, and change my clothes.

Communication

Take turns. Ask a partner questions to fill out the immigration form below with his or her information.

Department of Immigration PERMISSION TO ENTER
1. First name
2. Middle name
3. Family name
4. Date of birth
5. Place of birth
6. Nationality
7. Country of residence
8. Principal destination in this country
9. Hotel and/or street address
FORM 12a/PTO (Revised08) [Pursuant to Section 211(d)(3) of the IPA]

Goal 2 **Ask for and give personal travel information**

Work with a partner. Plan a trip. Tell your partner where you want to go, what you need to do before you travel, and when you want to travel.

▲ travel insurance

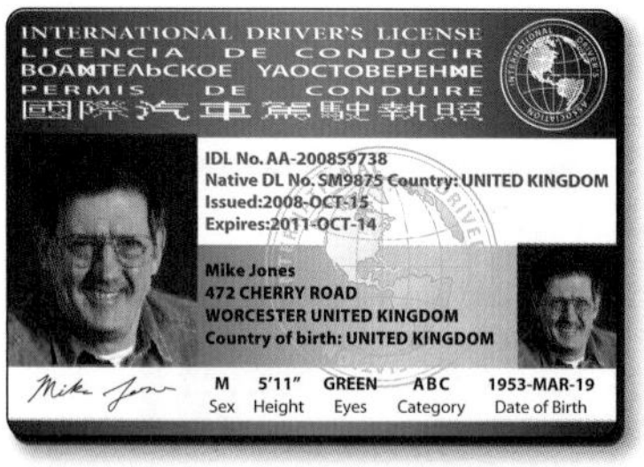

▲ international driver's license

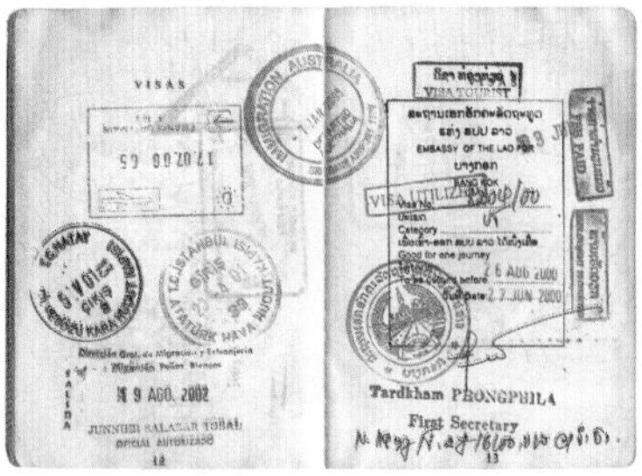
▲ visa

▲ passport

▲ airline ticket

Language Expansion: Travel documents and money

A. Complete the sentences. Use the names of the travel documents.

1. You need an ________________ to drive a car in a foreign country.
2. In some countries you need a ________________ to enter.
3. It's a good idea to buy ________________. Medical bills are expensive.
4. Your ________________ is your photo ID in any foreign country.
5. You can buy an ________________ on the Internet. But you need to write down or print the confirmation number.

B. Talk to a partner. What is the best form of money to take on your trip? Why?

Give an opinion

I think credit cards are good.

The best idea is to take . . .

Give a reason

People steal . . .

. . . don't accept . . .

People lose cash.

. . don't cash checks.

▲ credit cards

▲ traveler's checks

▲ checks

▲ cash

Grammar: *Should* for advice

Should

Subject	*should*	Adverb of frequency	Verb	Complement
You	should	(always)	make	a copy of your passport.
You	shouldn't		wear	expensive jewelry.

*We use *should/shouldn't* to give advice.

Questions with *should*

Should	Subject	Verb	Complement
Should	I	take	a taxi from the airport?

*We use questions with *should* to ask for advice.

A. Ask for advice. Write the questions.

1. **Q:** Should I take the shuttle bus to the airport?
   A: Yes, you should. The shuttle bus is quick and cheap.
2. **Q:** ______________________
   A: No, you shouldn't. It is hot at the beach. You don't need a sweater.
3. **Q:** ______________________
   A: Yes, you should. Credit cards are accepted in a lot of shops.
4. **Q:** ______________________
   A: No, you shouldn't. It's dangerous to carry cash.

B. Work with a partner. Take turns. Ask the questions in exercise **A** and give different advice. Use imperatives and *should.*

Conversation

A. Listen to the conversation. What does Claudia want from the United States?

Track 1-14

Mohammad: Hi, Claudia. You know the USA. Can you give me some advice? I'm going to New York in January.
Claudia: Lucky you! How can I help?
Mohammad: First. Should I buy travel insurance?
Claudia: Yes, you should. Hospitals and doctors are very expensive in the U.S.
Mohammad: OK. That's another $200. What about clothes? Should I take a coat?
Claudia: Definitely. It's very cold in January. You should take a warm sweater as well and some gloves and a scarf.
Mohammad: Mmm, that's another $100.
Claudia: Oh, just one more thing! Don't forget to buy me a nice present.
Mohammad: Oh no! That's another $500! Traveling is expensive.

B. Practice the conversation with a partner. Switch roles and practice it again.

Goal 3 Give travel advice

Take turns. Tell a partner where you want to go. Then give your partner travel advice. Use the conversation for ideas.

Reading

A. Answer the questions.

1. Do you think the author enjoys traveling? ______________________
____
____
2. Why should you check the expiration date of your passport? ______________________
____
____
3. Why should you tie a sock to your bags?
____
____
____
4. Why should you take a good book when you travel? ______________________
____
____
5. Write a list of snacks you would take when traveling by air. ______________________
____
____

Real Language

We use the expression *share some pointers* to say *give advice*.

Word Focus

expiration date = The *expiration date* of a document is the date it comes to an end or can no longer be used.

Smart Traveler

EXPERT OPINION

In his book Easy Travel, *Mike Connelly,* ***shares some pointers*** *on making travel easy:*

■ **DOCUMENTS** Make sure you have all your documents: passport, visas, tickets, traveler's checks, etc. You should always check the **expiration date** of your passport. Many countries won't let you enter with less than six months left on your passport. Don't forget to buy medical insurance. Medical bills can be very expensive, especially in the United States and Europe. Finally, you should make copies of all your important documents and credit cards and keep them in another bag.

■ **PACKING** My advice is—always travel light! I hate to carry heavy bags. Just take the minimum. There is an old saying: *Breakfast in Berlin. Dinner in Delhi. Bags in Bangkok!* So, don't pack anything important in your check-in bag; put important things in your carry-on bag. You don't want to arrive home without your house keys. Another tip—don't use expensive suitcases. People don't steal dirty old bags. Finally, here's a good little tip—tie a sock or brightly colored string to your bags. Why? So you can quickly see your bag on the baggage carousel.

■ **THE AIRPORT** My first piece of advice is that you should always carry a good book. It helps to pass the time as you wait for your delayed flight. Don't forget to take a sweater or a jacket on the plane. It can get very cold on a long night flight. And then there is airline food. Take a snack (cookies or fruit) with you. Sometimes the food is late, sometimes it doesn't arrive at all, and it's never very good.

B. Circle **T** for *true* and **F** for *false*.

1. You need a lot of documents to travel. T F
2. You need to take a lot of clothes in your bag. T F
3. Bags can be hard to identify at the airport. T F
4. Flights are never late. T F
5. Airplane food is always good. T F

Writing

Write some travel tips for your country. Think about the following topics:

- transportation
- how to carry money
- Can you drink the water?

Thailand is a safe country and the people are very friendly. But, like most places, you should be careful. Here are some tips:

- Taxis are cheap, but ask the price first.
- Many tourists use *tuk tuks*. However, they are dangerous. Be careful.
- Don't use the buses. They are slow and crowded.
- Don't carry a lot of money with you. Most shops accept credit cards.
- The water is not safe to drink, so you should buy water in bottles.
- Don't go out alone at night.

Have a nice stay!

Goal 4 **Share special travel tips with others**

Read your travel tips to a partner. Then share them with the class.

E VIDEO JOURNAL *BEAGLE PATROL*

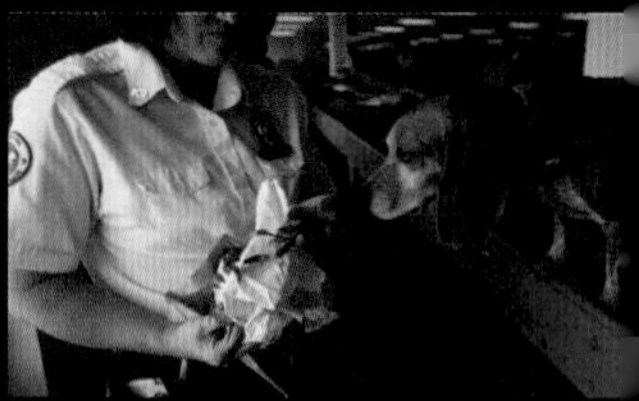

Before You Watch

A. Look at the photos. Do you have working dogs in your country? How do these dogs help us?

▲ guide dog

▲ sheepdog

▲ detector dog

▲ police dog

B. Study the words and the sentences. Then read the video summary. Use the words to complete the text.

disease **to bother** **illegal**

Rats are dirty. Sometimes they carry **disease**.
Hey kids! Please be quiet. I'm trying to work. You're **bothering** me.
You can't park your car there. It's not allowed. It's **illegal**.

Video summary

Airline passengers sometimes carry food, for example fruit, that may bring ____________________ into a country. Detector dogs can find this food by smelling the passengers' bags. Brent Heldt is training a dog called Stockton to be a detector dog. Stockton has to find the ____________________ food, but also he must not ____________________ the passengers.

While You Watch

A. Watch the video. Circle the names of things you see.

uniform	**apples**	**suitcase**	**passport**
gun	**orange**	**mango**	**beef jerky**

B. Watch the video again. Circle **T** for *true* and **F** for *false*.

1. Brent and Stockton play before they start work. T F
2. Detector dogs look for meat. T F
3. Stockton does not find the meat. T F
4. Stockton eats the meat he finds. T F
5. Stockton is learning slowly. T F

After You Watch

In the video we saw that dogs can be very useful in airports. Work with a partner to write a list of possible problems with dogs in airports.

Communication

Role-play the following situations.

Situation 1
Student A is a dog handler.
Student B is a passenger. The dog is sniffing your bag. You don't like dogs. In your culture dogs are dirty. Complain to the dog handler.

Situation 2
Student A is a passenger. The dog finds some fruit in your bag. It is a gift for your mother.
Student B is the dog handler. Explain that the passenger shouldn't bring fruit into the county. Take the fruit.

FOOD

1. Can you name any of the foods in the pictures?
2. What is your favorite food?

UNIT GOALS

Talk about food
Order a meal
Talk about diets
Discuss unusual and favorite foods

UNIT 4

Vocabulary

Talk to a partner. Choose a word or phrase from the box to describe each group of foods.

drinks dairy products vegetables fruit protein meat

Milk and Water are drinks.

Grammar: *Some* and *any* with count and non-count nouns

Count and non-count nouns	
Singular	**Plural**
This is a lemon.	Those are lemons.
This is milk.	~~Those are milks.~~

*For nouns you can count, we add *-s* or *-es* to form the plural.
*Nouns you cannot count don't have a plural form.

Some* and *any			
	Count nouns		**Non-count nouns**
	Singular	**Plural**	
Statement	We need an apple.	There are **some** oranges on the table.	There is **some** cheese on the table.
Negative	We don't have a lemon.	There aren't **any** bananas at the store.	We don't have **any** milk.
Question	Do we have a red pepper?	Are there **any** eggs?	Do you have **any** butter?

*You can also use *some* for questions with *would* and *could*.
Would you like **some** *apples?*
Could I have **some** *milk?*

A. Write the food words from the picture in the correct column.

Count nouns	Non-count nouns

B. Add other food words to the chart. Use your dictionary.

C. Complete the sentences with *a/an*, *the*, *some*, or *any*.

1. Do we have ____________ tomatoes?
2. There aren't ____________ eggs.
3. There is ____________ milk in the fridge.
4. I think ____________ cheese is on the table.
5. Pass me ____________ apple, please.

Conversation

Track 1-15

A. Listen to the conversation. What do you need to make a Spanish omelet?

Lee: Let's make a Spanish omelet.
Hyejin: Great. What do we need?
Lee: OK, it says here you need some olive oil. Do we have any olive oil?
Hyejin: No, we don't, but it doesn't matter; we have some corn oil. That will do.
Lee: Next, we need some potatoes, a large onion, and a red pepper.
Hyejin: We don't have a red pepper.
Lee: Never mind. We can use a green pepper.
Hyejin: OK. And then we need some eggs. Four eggs.
Lee: OK, let's begin!

Real Language

We can use *never mind* or *it doesn't matter* to show something is not important.

B. Practice the conversation with a partner. Switch roles and practice it again.

C. Choose a new recipe and repeat the conversation.

Word Focus

Names of fractions:
½ = one half
1/3 = one third
¼ = one fourth
or one quarter

Goal 1 Talk about food

Tell a partner the name of a food dish you like. Talk about the ingredients you need to make it.

B GOAL 2 ORDER A MEAL

Listening

Track 1-16

A. Listen to the **waiter** taking an order from **customers**. How many customers are there?

Track 1-16

B. Listen again and write the food and drink that each person ordered.

	Drink	Food
Man		
Woman		

Word Focus

waiter = A *waiter* is a person who works in a restaurant and serves food and drinks.

customer = A *customer* is a person who buys goods or services.

Menu

Appetizers

Chicken n' Cheese

Deep-fried chicken served with fresh tomatoes and sliced Cheddar cheese

Vegetable Soup

Made from fresh vegetables

Main Dishes

Seashore Pasta

Pasta served with salmon and broccoli in a cream sauce

Butter-Baked Chicken

Roasted half-chicken in a mushroom sauce, served with steamed carrots

Filet Mignon

8 oz. grilled tenderloin steak, served with Iceberg salad and your favorite salad dressing

Drinks

Fruit Cocktails, Non-Alcoholic Beer, Soda, Coffee

C. Listen again. Who asked these questions?

Track 1-16

1. Are you ready to order? waiter
2. Do you have any mineral water? ______
3. What would you recommend? ______
4. Does the filet mignon come with salad? ______
5. Anything else? ______

Pronunciation: Reduced forms *do you have* . . . and *would you like* . . .

Track 1-17

A. Listen to the full form and the reduced form.

Track 1-18

B. Listen and check (✓) the correct column. Then listen again and repeat.

	Full form	Reduced form
1. Do you have a pen?		
2. Would you like some more bread?		
3. Do you have any paper?		
4. Would you like a cup of coffee?		
5. Do you have any change?		

Do you have any oranges?

Would you like some milk?

Communication

Role-play the following situation.

Student A
You work in a food store. Serve the customer.

Student B
You want to make one of the dishes on page 41.
Ask for the food you need from the sales assistant.

✓ Goal 2 Order a meal

Work with a partner. Choose roles and role-play. Switch roles and role-play again.

Student A You are a customer in a restaurant. Order a meal from the menu on page 42.

Student B You are the waiter. Take the customer's order.

Language Expansion: Diets

Many people eat a special diet. Sometimes they go on a diet to lose weight and sometimes so that they will feel healthier. Here are two diets.

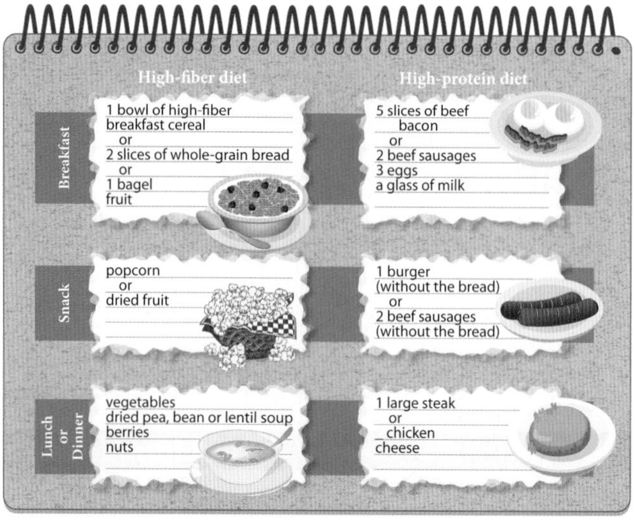

A. Write the names of these foods in the correct column.

▲ broccoli

▲ cauliflower

▲ baked beans

▲ bagels

▲ breakfast cereal

▲ nuts

▲ burger

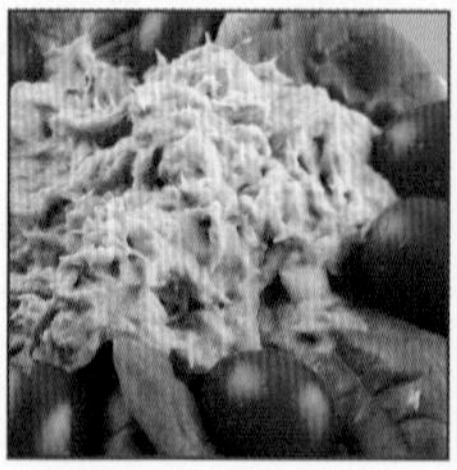
▲ tuna salad

High fiber	High protein

B. Add the names of other high-fiber and high-protein foods you know to the chart.

Grammar: *How much* and *how many* with quantifiers: *lots of, a few, a little*

	Information question	Quantifiers	
		++++	+
Count	**How many** oranges do you need?	I need **lots of** oranges.	I need **a few** oranges.
Non-count	**How much** milk do we have?	We have **lots of** milk.	We have **a little** milk.

*We use *lots of* and *a few* to answers questions about quantity.
*We use *a little* to answer questions about small quantities we cannot count.

A. Match the questions and the answers.

1. How many lemons do you want? ___
2. How much chicken should I buy? ___
3. How many heads of lettuce do we need? ___
4. How much sugar do you want? ___
5. How much water do you want? ___

a. We need a lot. We don't have any meat at home.
b. I'm not very thirsty. Just a little, please.
c. We have a lot of lemons. We only need a few.
d. Just one. We have a lot of salad.
e. Just a little. I don't like sweet coffee.

B. Fill in the blanks with *How much, How many, lots of, a few, a little.*

1. **Q:** How many potatoes would you like? **A:** Just a few, thanks.
2. **Q:** ______________ steak do we need? **A:** There are eight of us so we need ______________ steak.
3. **Q:** ______________ broccoli would you like? **A:** I'm not very hungry. Just ______________.
4. **Q:** ______________ apples do we need? **A:** We only need ______________. We already have some at home.

Conversation

A. Listen to the conversation. Can Pat eat popcorn?

Track 1-19

Kim: You're looking good.
Pat: Thanks, Kim. I'm on a special diet. It's a high-fiber diet.
Kim: High fiber? You mean lots of bread and fruit?
Pat: That's right.
Kim: How much bread can you eat for breakfast?
Pat: I can eat two slices of whole grain bread for breakfast or one bowl of high-fiber cereal.
Kim: And what about snacks?
Pat: No problem. I can eat lots of popcorn and dried fruit.
Kim: Mmm, sounds like a delicious diet. Maybe I'll join you.

B. Practice the conversation with a partner. Switch roles and practice it again.

Goal 3 Talk about diets

Repeat the conversation. Use the high-protein diet on page 44.

▲ laver on rocks in the Gower Peninsula, Wales

Reading

A. Look at the photos. Do people eat seaweed in your country?

B. Answer the questions.

1. What is lava bread made from? ______
2. Where is laver found? ______
3. What is seaweed used for in Japan? ______
4. What does the author order? ______
5. Would you like to eat seaweed? Give your reasons. ______

Word Focus

gelatinous = If something is *gelatinous,* it has a slightly rubbery, jelly-like texture.
delicacy = A *delicacy* is a food that is considered to be special, perhaps particularly tasty, rare, or expensive.

Cardiff, Wales

Eating Seaweed

▲ Welsh lava bread

I am sitting in a small café in Wales, reading through the menu. There are lots of familiar items, but something called *lava bread* catches my eye. I'm sure there aren't any volcanoes in Wales, so I can't think what *lava bread* could be.

I call the waitress over to help: apparently, *lava bread* is made from a type of seaweed called *laver*. It is found on the beaches along the Gower Peninsula. Once it has been collected, it is thoroughly washed, then boiled for several hours until it forms a **gelatinous** paste. This is then mixed with oatmeal, fried and then eaten for breakfast, or spread on hot buttered toast. Laver is very good for you because it is rich in many nutrients such as protein, iodine and vitamins.

This sounds to me as if it's quite similar to the seaweed which is considered a great **delicacy** in Japan. *Nori* are

▲ Japanese sushi rolls

thin sheets of dried seaweed which are used in many sushi dishes. *Wakame* is often used in soups such as miso. Having spent some time in Japan, I became very fond of these seaweed dishes, so I decide to try the Welsh *lava bread* and order a portion from the waitress.

▲ sushi sandwich

Writing

Write about your favorite food by answering the questions. Use the recipe below as a model.

- What is your favorite recipe?
- What are the ingredients?
- How do you make it?
- Do you eat it for breakfast, lunch, snack, or supper?

My favorite food is chicken pozole. It is a Mexican white-corn soup and it is delicious.

You need the following ingredients:
2 kilos chicken
½ kg canned hominy (white corn)
1 slice of onion
3 red chili peppers
1 head of garlic
1 teaspoon of cumin

Steps
1. Boil the chicken, slice of onion, and the head of garlic in 2 liters of water for 1 hour.
2. Cut the chicken into small pieces and return to the water.
2. Add the hominy, the ground red chili peppers, and the cumin. Cook for 15 minutes.
3. Serve with chopped lettuce, sliced radishes, chopped onion, cilantro, and lemon juice.

You can eat pozole at any time, but we usually eat it for supper.

▲ chicken pozole

▲ pozole ingredients

Goal 4 **Discuss unusual and favorite foods**

Tell a partner about your experiences eating unusual and favorite foods.

E VIDEO JOURNAL *DANGEROUS DINNER*

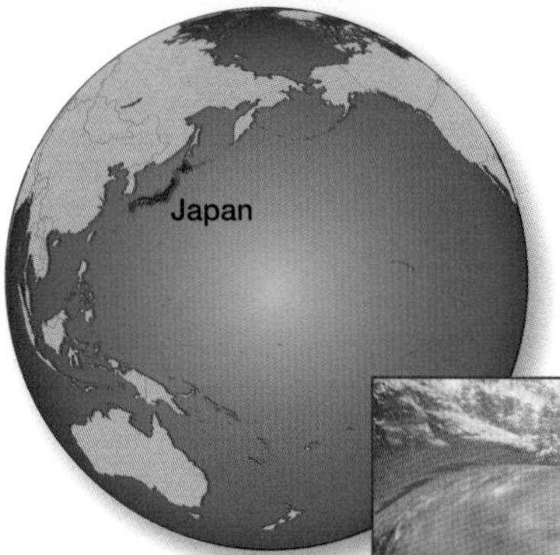

Before You Watch

Work with a partner. Discuss these questions.

1. Which of these fish can kill you?
2. How can they kill you?

▲great white shark

▲puffer fish

▲stone fish

▲sting ray

▲whale shark

While You Watch

A. Watch the video. Match the person with the comments.

1. Tom Cardonnam __
2. Chef Hayashi __
3. Hidenori Kadobayashi, Tokyo Health Department __
4. Yuji Nagashima, Tokyo University of Fisheries __

a. A tiger *fugu* has enough toxin to kill 30 people.
b. I can still breathe.
c. It'll be fine, don't worry.
d. About 70 percent of the poisonings happen in private homes.

B. Watch the video again. Circle **T** for *true* and **F** for *false*.

1. The puffer fish is not expensive. T F
2. Chef Hayashi has a license to prepare *fugu*. T F
3. About 30 people die every year because they eat *fugu*. T F
4. American General Douglas MacArthur introduced a test for *fugu* chefs. T F
5. Tom likes the *fugu*. T F

C. Answer the questions.

1. Is Tom worried about eating *fugu*?______________________________
2. Why did General Douglas MacArthur introduce a test for *fugu* chefs?
____
3. When did Chef Hayashi get his license? ______________________________
4. How does *fugu* poison kill a person? ______________________________
5. How many people can a tiger *fugu* kill? ______________________________

After You Watch

Discuss these questions with a partner.

1. Why do you think people like to eat *fugu*?
2. Would you eat *fugu*?

Communication

Read the menu. Take turns being a waiter and a customer at the Funky Food Restaurant.

Menu

Funky Food Restaurant

Ostrich Burger

Try our African Special.
Quarter pound $10
Half pound $15
Served with French fries and salad

Fugu

Prepared by our licensed chef
Small $50
Large $75

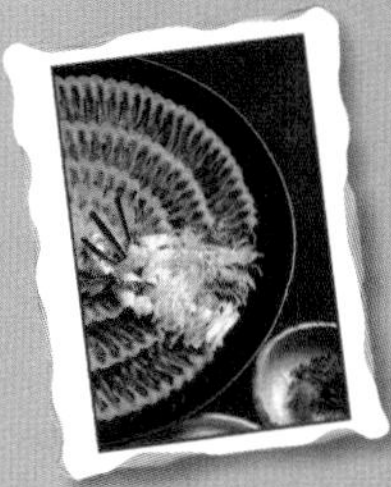

Pasta

Served in a cream sauce
Chicken $20
Salmon $35

▲ an ostrich

▲ pasta spirals

SPORTS

1. What are these sports?
2. What sports do you do? What sports would you like to do?

UNIT GOALS

Talk about activities happening now
Compare everyday and present-time activities
Talk about favorite sports
Discuss adventure holidays

UNIT 5

Vocabulary

A. Read the conversations. Use the words in **blue** to label the photos.

Anna is studying for a test. She is bored and tired, so she is calling some friends.

Anna:	Hi! What's up? What are you doing?
Bridget:	We're at the beach, Kenny's **swimming**, and the twins are **playing soccer**. How about you? What are you doing?
Anna:	I'm working! Grrrr!

Anna:	Hi Jill. What are you doing?
Jill:	I'm at the Extreme Sports Center with Amy and Pat. They're **climbing** and I'm **rappelling**. It's really cool. Why don't you come?
Anna:	I can't. I'm studying for the test.

Anna:	Hi Edith. What's happening?
Edith:	Hi. I'm at the gym. I'm **taking a break**. Mary and Jill are here too. Mary is **lifting weights** and Jill is **jogging**. What are you doing?
Anna:	I'm studying. Boring!!!

1. ________________

2. ________________

3. ________________

4. ________________

5. ________________

6. ________________

7. ________________

B. Take turns. Read the clues to a partner. Guess the activity. Write your answer.

1. You do this in the gym. ________________
2. You do this in a swimming pool. ________________
3. You play this with a ball. ________________
4. It is like running. ________________
5. You do this at home or in the library. ________________
6. You do this when you are tired. ________________

Grammar: Present continuous tense

Present continuous tense		
Statement	I **am playing** soccer	right now.
Negative	They **are not taking** a break	at the moment.
		now.
Yes/no question	**Are** you **studying**	right now?
Wh- question	What **are** you **doing**	at the moment?
		now?

*We use the present continuous tense to talk about things that are happening at the moment.

A. Complete the email. Remember to use the present continuous tense.

B. Ask a partner these questions.

What is Haroun doing?
What is Fethi doing?

Mail

New | Print | Delete | Move | Spell Check

TO:

CC:

BC:

Subject: (no subject)

What's up? Haroun and I are at the Cybercafe. Haroun ________ computer games as usual of course. I ________ some research for my project. It's a bit boring, so I ________ some emails.

Fethi

Send | Close

Conversation

A. Look at the picture and listen to the conversation. What are the twins doing?

Track 1-20

Mom: Hey, it's quiet today. Where are the kids?
Dad: Well, Mario's playing basketball in the yard.
Mom: What's Betty doing?
Dad: She's swimming in the pool.
Mom: And the twins? What are they doing?
Dad: Uhh. I don't know.
Mom: Hey, you two. What are you doing?
Twins: We're playing soccer.

B. Practice the conversation with a partner. Switch roles and practice it again.

C. Make a new conversation using other sports.

Goal 1 **Talk about activities happening now**

Talk to a partner. What are your family and friends doing now?

Listening

Track 1-21

A. Listen to the phone calls. The people are talking about ____.

a. what they usually do
b. what they are doing at the moment
c. both

▲ go ice skating

▲ go to the movies

▲ study

▲ play basketball

▲ go to a ball game

▲ fix the roof

Track 1-21

B. Listen again. What do these people usually do? When?

1. Allan and Karen always ______________ on ______________.
2. Dave always ______________ in the ______________.
3. Robin always ______________ on ______________.

Track 1-21

C. Listen again. What are they doing today?

1. Allan and Karen ______________________________.
2. Dave ______________________________.
3. Robin ______________________________.

Pronunciation: Reduced form of *what are you . . .*

Track 1-22

A. Listen to the full form and the reduced form.

What are you doing?

What are you eating?

Track 1-23

B. Listen and check (✓) the correct column.

	Full form	Reduced form
1. What are you reading?		
2. What are you thinking?		
3. What are you playing?		
4. What are you cooking?		
5. What are you writing?		

Track 1-23

C. Listen again. Repeat the sentences.

Communication

One member of the group mimes a sport. The other members of the group try to guess the sport.

Are you playing basketball?

No, I'm not.

Are you rock climbing?

Yes, I am.

✓ Goal 2 Compare everyday and present-time activities

Work with a partner. What are you doing now? What do you do at this time on a Sunday?

Language Expansion: Team sports and individual sports

A. Write the following sports in the correct box according to the categories.

baseball golf gymnastics football volleyball ice hockey diving skateboarding

	INDOOR ⬇	OUTDOOR ⬇
TEAM ➡	 1. ______ 2. ______	 1. ______ 2. ______
INDIVIDUAL ➡	 1. ______ 2. ______	 1. ______ 2. ______

Word Focus

We use *play* for team games—for example *I **play** soccer.*
We use *go* for individual sports—for example *I **go** swimming.*

B. Work in groups. Think of other ways to categorize sports. Prepare a chart with your new groups of sports. Have the other groups guess the names of your categories.

C. Write the names of more sports.

play	soccer,
go	swimming,

Grammar: Stative verbs

Stative verbs

like	Why do you **like** outdoor sports? I **like** to be outdoors.	know	You **know** I can't swim.
hate	I **hate** indoor sports.	want	I don't **want** to go bungee jumping.
think	I **think** indoor sports are boring.	need	You **need** a lot of equipment. The equipment is expensive.
prefer	Do you **prefer** outdoor sports?	cost	It **costs** a lot of money.

*We usually do not use stative verbs in the present continuous tense.

A. Circle the correct form of the verb in parentheses.

1. Skiing is expensive. It (is costing/costs) a lot of money.
2. I (am needing/need) a new soccer shirt.
3. The kids (are playing/play) in the garden at the moment.
4. I don't like team games. I (am preferring/prefer) outdoor sports.
5. Susan (is thinking/thinks) that all sports are boring.

Real Language

We say *me too* to agree with a positive statement and *me neither* to agree with a negative statement.

B. Write the correct form of the verb in parentheses.

1. Ashira ________________ (not like) to go swimming.
2. I ________________ (play) golf right now. Can I call you back?
3. I like rock climbing but my friend ________________ (think) I'm crazy.
4. Frederick can't come. He ________________ (fix) the car.
5. ________________ (you want) to go to the park?

Conversation

Track 1-24

A. Listen to the conversation. Does Adrian want to try rock climbing?

Adrian: Why do you like rock climbing?
Chris: I hate to be indoors all the time.
Adrian: Me too, but it looks dangerous. I don't want to die.
Chris: Me neither! That's why we use ropes.
Adrian: Do you need a lot of equipment?
Chris: Yes, you do and it costs a lot of money.
Adrian: So it's expensive and dangerous! Well, I think it's a crazy sport. Definitely not for me.

B. Practice the conversation with a partner. Switch roles and practice it again.

C. Change the sport and practice the conversation again.

Goal 3 **Talk about favorite sports**

Tell a partner about your favorite sport. Say why you like it.

Reading

A. Look at the photos. Where are the people? What are they doing?

____

____

____

____

Word Focus

look for = try to find

Vietnam

Climbing the Dragon's Spires

"What are you **looking for** up there?" asks Nguyen Mien, a Vietnamese fisherman.

"Nothing," I say. "I climb for fun."

It is difficult for a poor fisherman to understand why I am climbing the rock cliffs of Ha Long Bay in Vietnam. He works very hard and he has no time for sports. He lives on his fishing boat in a *floating village*. It isn't really a village because all the people live on boats. They move from one place to another. Nguyen catches **squid**, **shrimps**, and **crab**. He sells them to buy fresh water, vegetables, fuel, and clothes for his family.

So, what am I doing here? I am spending my vacation doing what I enjoy— rock climbing. Nguyen thinks I'm crazy, but I need some danger in my life.

B. Reread the article. Underline all the stative verbs.

C. Circle **T** for *true* or **F** for *false*.

1. Lynn is not a very good climber. T F
2. Nguyen Mien doesn't understand why Lynn is climbing the cliffs. T F
3. Nguyen Mien lives on his boat. T F
4. Lynn prefers fishing to rock climbing. T F
5. Nguyen Mien buys fresh water, vegetables, and fuel. T F

Writing

Read Saeed's email. Then write a similar email about another sport.

Mail

New Print Delete Move Spell Check

TO:

CC:

BC:

Subject: (no subject)

Hi, Pete.

Guess what? I'm joining the rock climbing club. It's cool. You know I don't like team games and I love to be outdoors, so this is the sport for me. The bad thing is the equipment is expensive.

Saeed

Send Close

Goal 4 Discuss adventure holidays

Talk with a partner. What type of adventure holiday would you like to take? Why?

E VIDEO JOURNAL *CHEESE-ROLLING RACES*

Before You Watch

A. Which of these unusual sports would you like to try? Why?

▲ octopush

▲ sumo wrestling

▲ sepak takraw

▲ cheese rolling

B. Match the words with the definitions.

1. cheese ___	a. unusual, mad
2. prize ___	b. when you hurt yourself
3. crazy ___	c. a person who watches a race
4. injury ___	d. a competition
5. a race ___	e. something you get when you win a race
6. spectator ___	f. a food made from milk

While You Watch

A. Fill in the blanks. Use the words in the box. Watch the video and check your answers.

injuries	**cold**	**spectators**	**winner**

1. The first ________________ of the day is Craig Brown.
2. One year, one of the cheeses rolled down the hill and went into the ________________.
3. It's not just spectators who get injured: competitors do as well, especially when it's ________________ or there hasn't been much rain.
4. Cheese-rolling spectator: "It's when the ground is really hard . . . that's when the ________________ are going to happen."

B. Watch the video again. Circle **T** for *true* and **F** for *false*.

1. Cheese rolling is an indoor sport. T F
2. The prize is a wheel of cheese. T F
3. The spectators sometimes get injured. T F
4. The cheese-rolling race is not dangerous. T F
5. Only British people can enter the cheese-rolling race. T F

After You Watch

Discuss these questions with a partner.

1. Why do you think people join the cheese-rolling race?
2. Do they want the cheese?
3. Do they want to have fun?
4. Are they crazy?

Communication

Role-play the following situation.

Student A is a competitor in the cheese-rolling race.

Student B interviews him/her.

Where do you come from?

Do you come every year?

Why do you come?

DESTINATIONS

1. Do you know the names of these places? Where are they?

2. Do you enjoy traveling? Why?

UNIT GOALS

Talk about past vacation trips
Exchange information about vacations
Use *was/were* to describe a personal experience
Talk about a discovery from the past

UNIT 6

Vocabulary

A. Match the photos to an activity from the box.

visit places of interest ___	**take photos**___
take a bus tour ___	**pack/unpack suitcases** ___
check into the hotel ___	**buy souvenirs** ___
rent a car ___	

1.

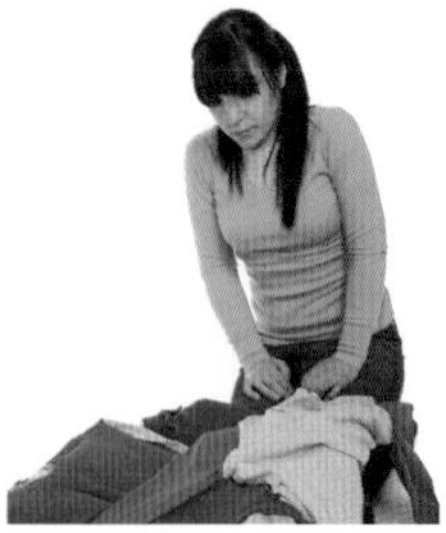
2.

3.

4.

5.

6.

7.

B. Which of these do you do *before* and *during* your vacation?

Before ____________________

During ____________________

C. Take turns. Tell a partner what other things you do before or during a vacation.

Grammar: Simple past tense

Simple past tense			
Statement	He **rented** a car on his trip to Europe last November.		
Negative	I **didn't have** a reservation yesterday.		
Yes/no questions	**Did they go** to Asia last year?		
Short answers	Yes, they **did**. No, they **didn't.**		
Information questions	Where **did** you **go** for your vacation last year?		
*We use the simple past tense to talk about completed actions or conditions.			
*Some verbs are regular in the simple past tense. They have an *-ed* ending.		*Some verbs are irregular in the simple past tense. They have many different forms.	
learn — learned arrive — arrived play — played ask — asked	travel — traveled want — wanted need — needed help — helped	agree — agreed buy — bought fly — flew know — knew go — went	tell — told leave — left say — said see — saw take — took

A. Complete the sentences. Use the simple past tense form of the verb in parentheses.

1. Last year, we __________ (visit) Machu Picchu in Peru.
2. We __________ (not, like) the hotel.
3. We __________ (buy) some interesting souvenirs.
4. When __________ (you arrive) at the airport?
5. We __________ (go) to Paris and Rome last year.

B. Unscramble the words to write questions and answers.

1. **Q:** to Europe Did you go year? last

   ____

2. **A:** to we No, went America.

   ____

3. **Q:** did buy you those Where souvenirs?

   ____

4. **A:** them bought in We Egypt.

   ____

Real Language

You can use the following expressions to show interest.

Informal ————————→ **Formal**

Wow! Sounds cool. Really! That's interesting.

Conversation

A. Listen to the conversation. How long did Maria stay in Cuzco?

Track 1-25

Christine: Hey, I love that poncho, Maria. Where did you buy it?
Maria: I bought it in Peru. We went to Peru for our vacation last year.
Christine: Wow! Sounds cool. Did you go to Lima?
Maria: No, we flew directly to Cuzco. We wanted to see the Inca ruins at Machu Picchu.
Christine: How long did you stay there?
Maria: We stayed for five nights.
Christine: Lucky you!

B. Practice the conversation with a partner. Switch roles and practice it again.

C. Practice the conversation again and change the underlined words using the information in the chart.

Country	Italy	United States	Great Britain
Capital	Rome	Washington, DC	London
Other City	Venice	Orlando	Edinburgh
Place of special interest	Doge's Palace	Disneyland	The Castle

Goal 1 Talk about past vacation trips

Take turns with a partner telling about a vacation you took.

B GOAL 2 EXCHANGE INFORMATION ABOUT VACATIONS

Listening

Track 1-26

A. Listen to the conversation. Circle the correct answer.

1. Glenn is telling his friend about _____.
   a. his vacation
   b. his hobby
   c. his work
2. His friend is ________.
   a. bored
   b. interested
   c. tired

Track 1-26

B. Listen again. Circle **T** for *true* or **F** for *false.*

1.	Glenn went to Oklahoma.	T	F
2.	He visited five theme parks.	T	F
3.	He didn't like Sea World.	T	F
4.	He went to the Harry Potter exhibition.	T	F
5.	He visited Islands of Adventure.	T	F

Pronunciation: Sounds of *-ed* endings

Track 1-27

A. Listen. Check the correct boxes. Then listen again and repeat.

	/d/	/t/	/id/
arrived	✓		
packed		✓	
visited			✓
rented			
liked			

Track 1-28

B. Listen to the sentences and check the pronunciation of the *-ed* ending.

	/d/	/t/	/id/
We **checked** into the hotel.			
I **packed** my bags.			
He **traveled** to Europe.			
They **stayed** at an expensive hotel.			

Track 1-28

C. Listen again and repeat the sentences.

Communication

Read your travel blog. Take turns with a partner asking each other questions about your vacation.

Where did you go next?

What did you do?

How long did you stay there?

Did you enjoy it? Why?

STUDENT A

From Zanzibar to Zebras **December 12th 2008**
Africa » Tanzania

Day 1 Arrived in Dar es Salaam. Checked in to hotel. Went swimming.
Day 2 Took boat to the island of Zanzibar.
Days 3-5 Sunbathed on the beach. Went diving.
Day 6 Flew to Arusha. Saw Kilimanjaro. It's BIG!
Days 7-10 Took a safari tour. Saw hundreds of wild animals. Took lots of photos.
Day 11 Returned to Arusha. Bought souvenirs. Took plane to Dar es Salaam and then flew home. Great holiday.

Read full story | Subscribe

STUDENT B

Mexico: Beaches and Pyramids **December 18th 2008**
Mexico » Mexico City » Cancun » Tulum » Oaxaca

Day 1 Arrived in Mexico City. Took subway to Chapultepec Park. Went to zoo.
Day 2 Rented a car. Visited the pyramid of the Sun and the Moon.
Days 3-5 Flew to Cancun. Went to beach.
Day 6 Visited ruins at Tulum. Watched traditional show.
Day 7 Colonial city of Oaxaca. Took a tour of the city. Drank hot chocolate in market.
Day 8 Returned to Mexico City. Flew home.

Read full story | Subscribe

Goal 2 Exchange information about vacations

Join another pair of students. Tell them about your partner's vacation from the activity above.

Language Expansion: Emphatic adjectives

Adjectives	Emphatic adjectives
good/nice	excellent outstanding magnificent amazing
bad	awful terrible horrible
interesting	fascinating
tiring	exhausting
dirty	filthy
clean	spotless
big	enormous huge

A. Write an emphatic adjective below each picture.

__________ __________ __________ __________ __________

B. Use emphatic adjectives to complete the text.

We had an __________ vacation. We visited six European countries in six days. My favorite country was Italy. Rome is a __________ city. There is so much to see: museums, architecture, ruins. We stayed in a __________ hotel. Everything about it was perfect. It had an __________ swimming pool and very friendly people.

Grammar: Simple past tense of *to be*

Simple past tense of *to be*	
Statement	I **was** exhausted.
Negative	The food **wasn't** great.
Information questions	Why **was** your vacation awful?
Yes/No Questions	**Were** they tired?
Short answers	No, they **weren't**.

A. Match the questions and the answers.

1. Were you tired? ___
2. Where were they? ___
3. Was the weather good? ___
4. Was he late? ___
5. Were the rooms clean? ___

a. No, he wasn't. He was on time.
b. They were in Peru.
c. No, they weren't. They were filthy.
d. Yes, I was. I was exhausted.
e. Yes, it was.

B. Complete the sentences with *was* or *were*.

1. We didn't enjoy our vacation. The weather ________________ very bad.
2. How ________________ the food?
3. ________________ you tired when you got home?
4. I ________________ really interested in the ruins. They were boring.
5. ________________ the hotel clean?

Conversation

A. Listen to the conversation. What was good about the vacation?

Track 1-29

Gill: How was your vacation?
Mike: It was terrible.
Gill: Why? What happened?
Mike: Well, first of all the weather was bad. It rained nonstop for two weeks.
Gill: Oh, no.
Mike: And the hotel was dirty. It was full of cockroaches.
Gill: Yuck! And how was the food?
Mike: Actually, the food was good.
Gill: Well, at least you enjoyed something.
Mike: Not really. I had a bad stomach and couldn't eat. Some vacation!

B. Practice the conversation with a partner. Switch roles and practice it again.

C. Practice again and change the underlined adjectives with emphatic adjectives.

Goal 3 **Use *was/were* to describe a personal experience**

Tell a partner about a good or bad experience you had.

The weather was awful.

The food was excellent.

Reading

A. Look at the photo of Hiram Bingham. Is he on vacation? What is he doing?

▲ Hiram Bingham

B. Read the article. Underline the emphatic adjectives.

C. Answer the questions.

1. Did Hiram Bingham discover Inca ruins in Ollantaytambo? ____________________
2. How much did he pay Arteaga? ______
3. Was the climb to Machu Picchu easy? ____________________
4. Where did they eat? ______________
5. How did the Incas cut the stones? ____________________

The City of Machu Picchu, the Cradle of the Inca Empire

Most people travel for vacations, but some people travel to explore and discover new places. In 1911, Hiram Bingham, an American archaeologist, traveled to Peru where he discovered Machu Picchu, the lost city of the Incas. Read his report of the discovery.

In 1911, I went to Cuzco in Peru looking for ancient Inca ruins. We left Cuzco and traveled to the modern city of Urubamba and then continued down the Urubamba River until we came to the beautiful little town of Ollantaytambo with its amazing Inca **fortress.** At this point we entered the Urubamba **gorge** and the journey became more difficult. However, we continued down the river and six days after we left Cuzco, we arrived at a place called Mandorpampa. A man came and introduced himself as Arteaga and I asked him about ruins. He told us of some ruins called Machu Picchu, 2,000 or more feet above the valley floor. I offered to pay him 50 cents per day to take us to the ruins and he agreed.

The next day, we crossed the river on a bridge made from four tree **trunks** and began an exhausting climb. At noon we arrived at a little grass hut. The **occupants** were very friendly and gave us some boiled potatoes and a gourd of cool water. The view was magnificent, the water was delicious, and the shade of the hut was agreeable, but there were no ruins. However, we continued upwards, sometimes climbing **ladders**, until at last we arrived in a **tropical forest** on top of the mountain.

Immediately we found some ancient Inca walls made of white stone. I knew at once that this was a truly amazing discovery.

I returned to Machu Picchu in 1912 and we began to clear the forest. The ruins started to appear and they were outstanding. The walls are made from enormous stones and they **fit** together perfectly. As we continued to clear the forest, we discovered more and more ruins, until at last the lost city of Machu Picchu stood before us.

The walls are made from enormous stones. The Incas had no metal tools, and no one knows how they cut the stones. We started to dig up the floor of the building but we didn't find anything of interest.

Word Focus

occupants = The *occupants* of a house are the people that live there.
fit = If something *fits*, it is the right shape and size.

Writing

Read the postcard. Write a similar postcard about your last vacation or one of the vacations on page 67.

Hi everyone,

Greetings from Phuket. We're having a great time here. We arrived in Bangkok last Saturday and we went to The Grand Palace. It was fascinating. There were some enormous statues. The hotel was spotless and the food was excellent, but the traffic was terrible. It is much more relaxing here on the beach in Phuket.

Love
G&D

Goal 4 **Talk about a discovery from the past**

Talk to a partner about another discovery from the past that you have read or heard about.

E VIDEO JOURNAL *MACHU PICCHU*

Before You Watch

A. Which of these beaches would you like to visit? Why?

Word Focus

Cuzco is also spelled Cusco.

B. Fill in the blanks. Use the words in the box to complete the video summary.

tourists	environment	quiet	business

Video summary

When Hiram Bingham discovered Machu Picchu it was a ______________ place. Now, many ______________ go to Machu Picchu every day. Some people say it is good for ______________, but other people say it is bad for the ______________.

While You Watch

A. Watch the video. Circle **T** for *true* and **F** for *false*.

1. Machu Picchu is a popular tourist destination. T F
2. Machu Picchu is sometimes known as the Lost Town of the Incas. T F
3. Conservationists think tourism is good for Machu Picchu. T F
4. Jose wants more people to come to Machu Picchu. T F

B. Watch again. Fill in the numbers and dates.

1. Machu Picchu is nearly ________________ feet up in the Andes.
2. Machu Picchu is more than ________________ years old.
3. Hiram Bingham found Machu Picchu in ________________.

C. Answer the questions.

1. What is Julio's job? ________________
2. What is Jose's job? ________________
3. What jobs do the people of Aguas Calientes do? ________________

After You Watch

Discuss these questions with a partner.

1. What are the big tourist attractions in your country?
2. Are there any problems with tourism in your country?
3. What are they?

Communication

A. Check (✓) the correct boxes.

	Advantage (+)	Disadvantage (–)
1. Tourism is good for business.	☐	☐
2. Tourists do not respect the local culture.	☐	☐
3. Tourists cause environmental damage.	☐	☐
4. Tourism helps people understand other cultures.	☐	☐

B. Discuss the question. Give examples.

Is tourism good or bad?

Tourists buy presents and stay in hotels.

That's good. It brings money to the country.

COMMUNICATION

1. Look at the pictures. What do they have in common?

2. What other ways do people communicate?

UNIT GOALS

Talk about personal communication
Give and write down contact details
Describe characteristics and qualities
Compare different types of communication

UNIT 7

Vocabulary

A. Label the pictures. Use the words in the box.

email	**fax**	**BlackBerry®**
TV	**text message**	**newspaper ad**
letter	**phone**	

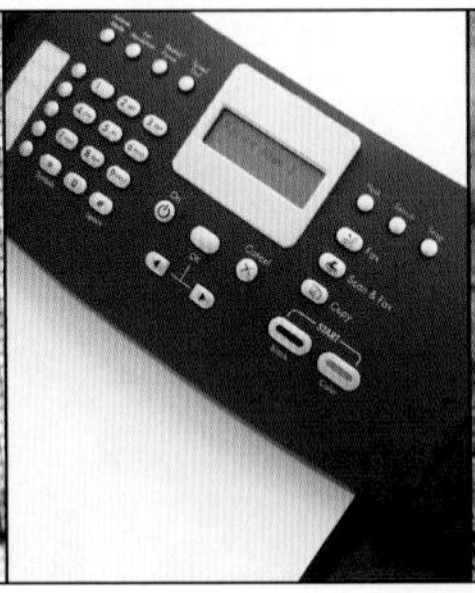

1. ______ 2. ______ 3. ______ 4. ______

5. ______ 6. ______ 7. ______ 8. ______

B. Write the words in exercise **A** in the correct column.

	Inexpensive	**Expensive**
fast		*phone call*
slow	*letter*	

Grammar: Verbs with direct and indirect objects

(Subject) + verb	**Indirect object**	**Direct object**
I sent	Mike	an email.
My parents bought	me	a BlackBerry®.
I wrote	Helen	a text message.
Find	me	his number, please.
I faxed	him	the diagram.
Give	me	a call.

Irregular past tense	
Present	**Past**
buy	bought
send	sent
write	wrote
find	found
get	got

A. Unscramble the words to write sentences.

1. sent a I fax Zeinab. ______________________
2. sent My brother an me email. ______________________
3. address. me his Find email ______________________
4. new Adnan a computer. I bought ______________________
5. a your mom Give call. ______________________

B. Read the situations and make requests. Use the verbs in parentheses.

	Situation	**Request**
1.	You lost your friend's phone number.	(send) Please send me your phone number.
2.	You want your friend to call you.	(give) ______________________
3.	You want your parents to buy you a printer.	(buy) ______________________
4.	You ask if you can pay someone by check.	(write) ______________________
5.	You want your friend to fax you a chart.	(fax) ______________________

Conversation

Track 2-2

A. Listen to the conversation. How did Ken communicate with Chris?

Tariq: Hey, Chris. I sent you an email yesterday and you didn't answer.
Chris: Email? What email? You didn't send me an email.
Tariq: Come on! You got it. Then I sent you a text message.
Chris: Text message? What text message? You didn't send me a text message, either. Honest!
Tariq: OK, well you've got no excuses now. Where's the $15 you owe me?
Chris: $15? What $15?

Real Language

We can use *Come on!* to show impatience.

B. Practice the conversation with a partner. Switch roles and practice it again.

C. Practice the conversation again. Change the underlined words.

Goal 1 | Talk about personal communication

Write a list of all the types of personal communication that you use. Compare it with your partner's list.

B GOAL 2 GIVE AND WRITE DOWN CONTACT DETAILS

Listening

Track 2-3

A. Listen to the radio program. Circle the correct answer.

This is a ___.
a. talk show
b. news program
c. phone-in program

Track 2-3

B. Listen again and complete the chart.

Telephone number	
Fax number	
Email address	
Text message address	
Mailing address	

Pronunciation: Endings *-ty* and *-teen*

Track 2-4

A. Listen and circle the word you hear.

1.	thirty	thirteen
2.	forty	fourteen
3.	fifty	fifteen
4.	sixty	sixteen
5.	seventy	seventeen
6.	eighty	eighteen
7.	ninety	nineteen

Track 2-5

B. Listen and repeat the numbers.

thirty	**sixteen**
thirteen	**seventy**
forty	**seventeen**
fourteen	**eighty**
fifty	**eighteen**
fifteen	**ninety**
sixty	**nineteen**

Communication

A. Write your contact information in column 1 of the chart.

B. Ask three of your classmates for their contact information. Complete the chart.

	Me	Classmate 1	Classmate 2	Classmate 3
Name				
Home phone number				
Fax number				
Cell phone number				
Email address				
Mailing address				

Real Language

We say *sorry, I missed that* or *could you repeat that, please* when we want someone to repeat something.

Goal 2 **Give and write down contact details**

Give the contact details of a friend or family member to a partner.

Language Expansion: The senses

The senses are the physical abilities of:

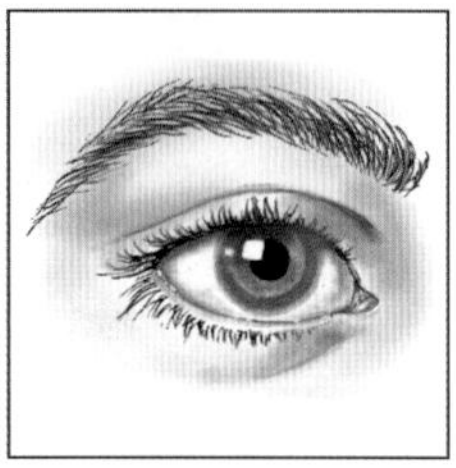
▲ sight

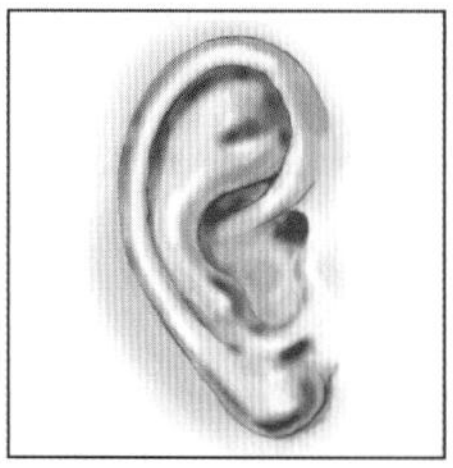
▲ hearing

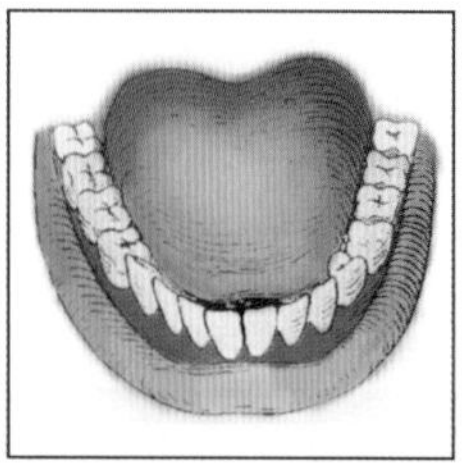
▲ taste

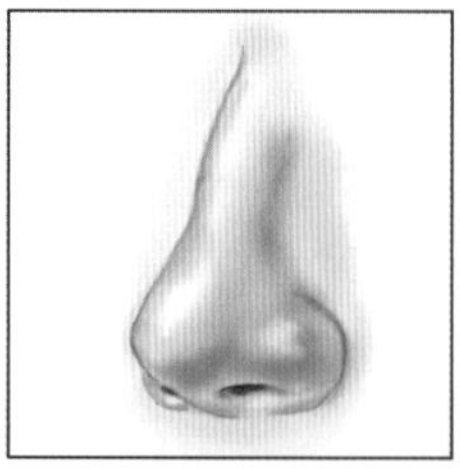
▲ smell

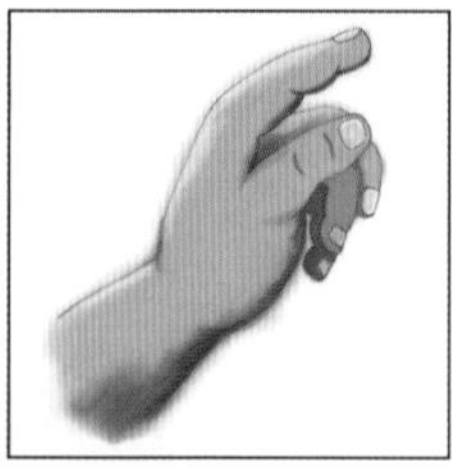
▲ touch

With the senses we perceive (*see, notice, feel*) characteristics and qualities of people, animals, places, and things.

A. Discuss this question with a partner. What senses do you use to identify these characteristics?

▲ sweet

▲ dirty

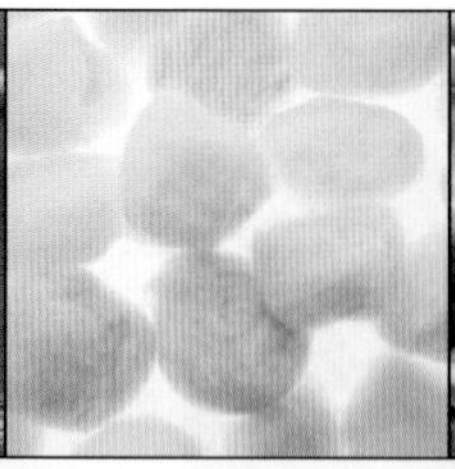
▲ soft

▲ salty

▲ loud

▲ bad

▲ green

▲ wet

B. Work with a partner to make a list of other things you can perceive with your senses.

Grammar: Linking verbs

Linking verbs		
Subject +	**verb +**	**adjective**
The food	**smells**	delicious.
It	**feels**	soft.
You	**look**	cold.
It	**tastes**	salty.
He	**sounds**	tired.

*Verbs of the senses are *not* action verbs.
*They are usually followed by an adjective.
*They are not used in the simple progressive tense.

A. Complete the sentences with linking verbs.

1. That washing machine can't be OK. It __________ very old.
2. Did you wash the car? It still ____________ dirty.
3. What are you cooking? It _____________ delicious.
4. I don't like this part of the city. It ___________ dangerous.
5. Hey, you changed your hair. It ____________ much better.
6. I don't like these French fries. They __________ too salty.
7. I prefer this sweater. It ____________ soft.
8. The mechanic says he fixed the rattle in the car, but it _____________ worse.

B. Take turns. Describe the pictures on page 80 by making statements with *looks, sounds, tastes, smells, feels,* and an adjective.

Conversation

Track 2-6

A. Listen to the conversation. What's wrong with the man's car?

Susan: Your car sounds strange.
Bill: I know. It started last week, but now it sounds worse.
Susan: I think it's the brakes.
Bill: It does feel funny when I use the brakes.
Susan: You should take it to the mechanic.
Bill: Maybe next week.
Susan: Go soon. New brakes are expensive.

B. Practice the conversation with a partner. Switch roles and practice it again.

Goal 3 Describe characteristics and qualities

Work with a partner. Use linking sense verbs to describe your classroom and your classmates.

Reading

A. How do dolphins communicate? Read the article and find out.

Word Focus

aquarium = a place where people pay to look at fish
tank = a glass box
clap = when you *clap* something, you bring it together quickly and firmly
raise = lift

B. Answer the questions.

1. What senses do dolphins use to communicate? ____________________
2. What do dolphins *talk* about? ________
____
3. Why is it difficult to understand dolphin communication? ________________
____
4. Do scientists understand everything that dolphins *say*? ________________
____
5. How do other animals communicate? Give some examples. ______________
____
____

The Secret Language of Dolphins

A mother dolphin talks to her baby . . . by telephone! The special call was made in an **aquarium** in Hawaii, where the mother and her two-year-old baby swam in separate **tanks**.

"It seemed clear that they knew who they were talking to," says Don White. But what did they say? Scientists are studying dolphins all over the world to understand their secret language. They don't understand everything yet, but they're listening . . . and learning.

Scientists think dolphins *talk* about everything, even such things as their age and how they are feeling. Scientists think that dolphins say things like "there are some good fish over here," or "watch out for that shark because he's hunting." "Sometimes one dolphin will speak and then another will seem to answer," says Sara Waller, who studies bottlenose dolphins off the California coast. Sometimes they all talk at the same time—like people at a party.

It is difficult to study *dolphin speak* in the sea because dolphins swim very quickly. Also, it seems that one sound can mean many different things. For example, when they are fighting, dolphins **clap** their mouths to say "go away!" But they make the same sound when they are playing. It's like humans. When you **raise** a hand, it might mean *hello*, *good-bye*, or *stop*.

Scientists still don't understand everything dolphins *say* but one day, who knows, maybe you'll get a phone call from a dolphin.

Writing

A. Writing text messages is slow so people use abbreviations. Can you read and understand these messages?

HI. HRU?
NOTHING. WANNA GO OUT TN?
Y?
OK LMK

GREAT. WRUD?
IDUNNO
GOTTA FINISH MY PROJECT
OK CU LATER

TEXTING GLOSSARY

2MOR	Tomorrow	NSISR	Not sure if spelled right
ASAP	As soon as possible	NVM	Never mind
B4N	Bye for now	OIC	Oh, I see
BCOS	Because	PLMK	Please let me know
BDAY	Birthday		
CU	See you	RU?	Are you?
DTS	Don't think so	THX	Thanks
FBM	Fine by me	WDYT?	What do you think?
GTG	Got to go		
HRU?	How are you?	WRUD	What are you doing?
IDTS	I don't think so		
IDUNNO	I don't know	WU?	What's up?
LMK	Let me know	Y?	Why?
LTNS	Long time no see		

B. Write a conversation with no abbreviations. Then write it as a text message. Give it to a partner to read.

Goal 4 **Compare different types of communication**

Work with a partner. Compare human communication with animal communication. How are they the same? How are they different? Share your ideas with the class.

E VIDEO JOURNAL *WILD ANIMAL TRACKERS*

Before You Watch

A. How can we communicate without using words? One way is to use small pictures or icons. What do these icons mean?

____________ ____________ ____________ ____________

B. Match the words to the definitions.

1. conservationist ___
2. increase ___
3. decrease ___
4. to track ___

a. to follow wild animals
b. a person who protects wild animals
c. to get (or make) bigger
d. to get (or make) smaller

While You Watch

A. Watch the video. Circle **T** for *true* and **F** for *false*.

1. In the video, you see lions. T F
2. Louis Liebenberg is trying to collect information about the animals. T F
3. The Bushmen and the conservationists speak the same language. T F
4. The small computer that the Bushmen use is called the Cyber Tracker. T F
5. Louis Liebenberg makes maps from the information. T F

B. Watch the video again and circle the correct answer.

1. The conservationists use Bushmen because ____.
   a. they are good trackers
   b. they can't read or write
   c. both of the above
2. The Bushmen collect information about ____.
   a. animals
   b. plants
   c. both of the above
3. The Cyber Tracker project started ____.
   a. 5 years ago
   b. 10 years ago
   c. 15 years ago

▲ A Bushman studies animal tracks in the mud.

After You Watch

The Cyber Tracker is a very quick way of recording information about wild animals. Can you think of other uses for the Cyber Tracker? Discuss it with a partner.

Communication

In some languages people use small pictures (pictograms) instead of letters to write. For example, in ancient Egyptian hieroglyphics:

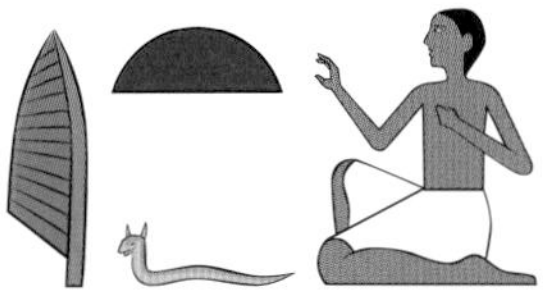 = father

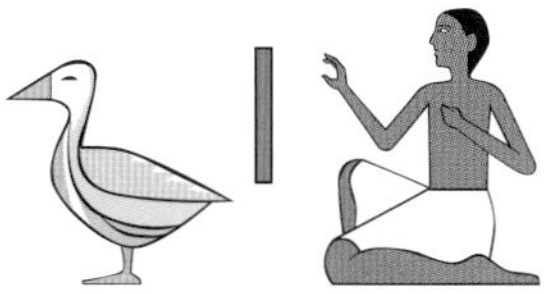 = son

A. Invent your own pictograms. Write a short message using your pictograms, not words.

B. Exchange your pictogram messages with a partner. Read your partner's message. Do you understand it?

THE FUTURE

1. Which of these events are in your future?
   a. buying a new car
   b. graduating from school
   c. getting married
   d. taking a trip

2. Are you looking forward to these events? Why?

UNIT GOALS

Talk about plans
Discuss long- and short-term plans
Make weather predictions
Discuss the future

UNIT 8

Vocabulary

A. Number the pictures to match phrases from the box.

1. study for the next test	**4. buy a new car**	**7. buy my own house**
2. get a new job	**5. have children**	**8. speak English fluently**
3. do the laundry	**6. clean the house**	

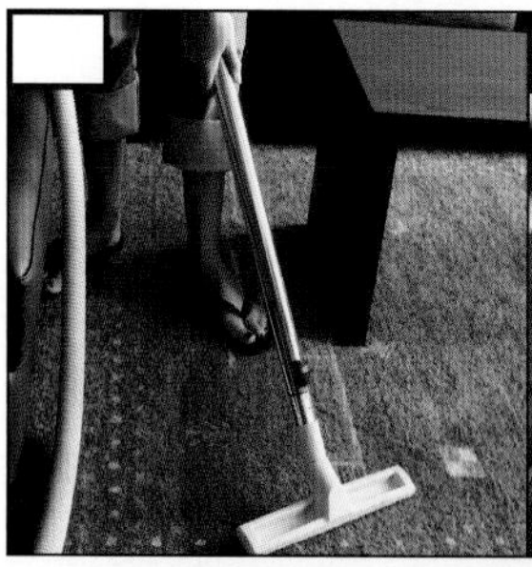

B. Write the plans from exercise **A** in the correct column.

Short-term plans	Long-term plans

I don't want to have children now. I'm too young.

I need to buy a new car. My car is really old.

C. Number the long-term plans in order of importance for you (1 for the most important plan). Compare your list with a partner's list. Give reasons.

Grammar: *Be going to*

Be going to	
Statement	We**'re going to** buy a new car tomorrow.
Negative	He**'s not going to** get a new job next year.
Yes/no question	**Are** you **going to** do the laundry this weekend?
Wh- question	When **are** you **going to** pay the phone bill?
*We use *be going to* to talk about our plans for the future.	

A. Match the questions and the answers.

1. Where are you going to have lunch today? ___
2. Are you going to invite Adnan to the meeting? ___
3. What are you going to do on Saturday? ___
4. When is Nicola going to arrive? ___
5. Is it going to rain this evening? ___

a. Yes, I am. He would like to come.
b. Maybe. I would take an umbrella.
c. At Luigi's.
d. We're going to go ice skating.
e. Her plane arrives at five o'clock.

B. Unscramble the words to write sentences. Number the sentences to make a conversation.

___. are going Who to meet? you

___. to a restaurant. to going go I'm

___. going my cousins. I'm meet to

___. you going this evening? to do What are

Real Language

We can say *mmm* or *I'm not sure* to show uncertainty.

Conversation

A. Listen to the conversation. Is Kiri going to go to the beach?

Track 2-7

Vera: Hi Kiri. What are you going to do this weekend?
Kiri: Well, I'm going to study for the test and do the laundry. Why do you ask?
Vera: We're going to go to the beach. Do you want to come?
Kiri: Mmm, I'm not sure. I'd love to but, . . . you know . . . work.
Vera: Danny is going to be there.
Kiri: Oh, I see. Well, maybe I can study for the test tonight. And I can do the laundry when we come back.
Vera: So, you're going to come?
Kiri: Sure!

B. Practice the conversation with a partner. Switch roles and practice it again.

C. Change the underlined words and practice it again.

Goal 1 **Talk about plans**

Tell a partner your plans for this weekend.

Listening

Track 2-8

A. Listen to the interview with a pop singer. Is he talking about his short-term plans or long-term plans?

Track 2-8

B. Listen again and circle **T** for *true* and **F** for *false*.

1. Pete is going to record his new album in June. T F
2. Pete is going to do a world tour this year. T F
3. Babs is going to have a baby in May. T F
4. The baby isn't going to change Pete's life. T F
5. Pete is going to start making a film at the end of the year. T F

Pronunciation: Reduced form of *going to*

Track 2-9

A. Listen to the sentences.

1. I'm going to buy a new computer.
2. Are you going to come?

Track 2-10

B. Listen to the sentences and check (✓) the box.

	Full form	Reduced form
1. When are you going to finish?	☐	☐
2. They're not going to like it.	☐	☐
3. We're going to leave at three thirty.	☐	☐
4. I'm going to take a shower.	☐	☐
5. Are you going to take a taxi?	☐	☐

Track 2-10

C. Listen again and repeat the sentences.

Communication

A. What are your short-term and long-term plans? Check (✓) the correct column.

Short-term plans **Are you going to . . .**	**Yes, I am.**	**I'm not sure.**	**No, I'm not.**
eat out tonight?			
go to a party this weekend?			
play or watch a sport this evening?			
rest this weekend?			

Long-term plans **Are you going to . . .**	**Yes, I am.**	**I'm not sure.**	**No, I'm not.**
start your own business?			
learn another language?			
move to another country?			
buy a new car?			

B. Take turns asking and answering the questions in exercise **A** Then ask a *wh-* question.

Are you going to eat out tonight?

Yes, I am.

Where are you going to go?

I'm not sure. Maybe to an Italian restaurant.

Goal 2 **Discuss long- and short-term plans**

Tell a partner your plans for tonight and your plans for the next five years.

◀ umbrella

◀ sunglasses

◀ rubber boots

◀ raincoat

◀ swimsuit

◀ scarf

◀ sweater

◀ sun hat

Language Expansion: Weather conditions

◀ windy, breezy

◀ cold, cool

◀ rainy, wet

◀ sunny, bright

◀ cloudy, dull, overcast

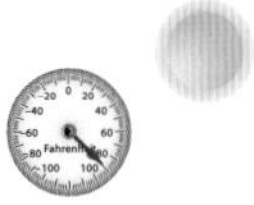
◀ hot, warm

We use adjectives to describe the weather.
Today is ***sunny*** *and* ***warm****.*

A. Complete the sentences. Use words from the box and the pictures.

1. It's not going to rain tomorrow. You don't need to take your ________________ and your ________________.
2. You should put on your sweater. It's going to be________________ outside.
3. The weather forecast says it's going to be cloudy today. You don't need to take your ________________.
4. It's going to be ________________ and ________________ tomorrow, so don't forget your sun hat.

B. Take turns. Make predictions about the weather. Tell a partner how to dress for it.

Grammar: *Will* for predictions

Will	
Statements	I think it **will** rain this afternoon. It **will** be windy tomorrow.
Negatives	Don't take your sweater. I'm sure it **won't** be cold.
Yes/no questions	**Will** it be windy?

*We use *be going to* and *will* to make predictions.
*We only use *will* when we decide on an immediate plan .
*I'**ll** answer the phone.*

A. Rewrite the sentences using *be going to* or *will*.

	Be going to	***Will***
1.	I think it's going to rain tomorrow.	I think it will rain tomorrow.
2.	______________	I'm sure it won't be sunny this afternoon.
3.	Are temperatures going to rise in the next 100 years?	______________
4.	______________	What will the weather be like on the weekend?
5.	Is it going to be overcast tomorrow?	______________

B. Write statements that are true for you. Use *be going to* or *will*.

Conversation

Track 2-11

A. Listen to the conversation.

Andrew: Do we have everything ready for the beach?
Barbara: Sure. Everything's ready.
Andrew: Do you think it's going to rain?
Barbara: No, they say it's going to be hot.
Andrew: Are you going to take your umbrella?
Barbara: No, I said it's going to be hot. It's not going to rain.
Andrew: No, I mean your beach umbrella for the sun.
Barbara: Oh, I see. Yes, that's a good idea.

B. Practice the conversation with a partner. Switch roles and practice it again.

C. Circle the predictions. Change the predictions to *will* and practice it again.

Goal 3 Make weather predictions

Talk to a partner. What is the weather like now? What is it going to be like tomorrow?

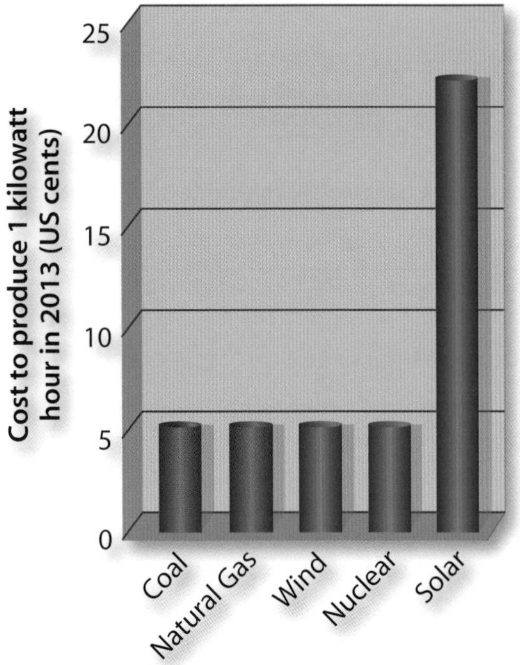

Reading

A. Discuss these questions with a partner. Read the article to check your answers.

1. What are fossil fuels?
2. What is alternative energy?

B. Underline the sentences in the article that contain *will*. Rewrite them using *be going to*.

C. Answer the questions.

1. Why did the author put solar panels on his roof? ______________________
2. In 2100, the world's energy will be equal to how many light bulbs per person? ______________________
3. What are three problems with solar power? ______________________ ______________________
4. What are two problems with wind energy? ______________________
5. Does Michael Pacheco think there will be enough energy in the future? ______________________

Future Energy

WHERE WILL WE GET OUR ENERGY?

It's a bright sunny day. I put the last solar panel on my roof, I switch it on, and I have electricity. I'm free! Now, I won't have to worry about electric bills or oil prices, and I won't feel guilty about pollution. But what's this? A cloud passes in front of the sun and my lights go out! I'm going to have to start my generator and burn some more gasoline. This isn't going to be easy after all.

We are going to have a big energy problem in the future. Today, the world uses 320 billion kilowatt-hours of energy a day. That's equal to about 22 light bulbs burning nonstop for every person on the planet. By 2100 we will use three times as much energy. How will we get the energy? At the moment, we get most of our energy from fossil fuels: coal, oil, and natural gas. But fossil fuels are dirty and they will not last forever. In the long term, we will have to find **alternatives**. We will need **renewable** energy.

SOLAR POWER

On a cloudy day near the city of Leipzig in the former East Germany, I walked across a field with 33,500 solar panels. It produces enough energy for 1800 homes.

One problem with solar power is that it is expensive, but the cost of solar will fall as technology improves. "Thirty years ago it was **cost-effective** on satellites," says Daniel Shugar, president of PowerLight Corporation. "Today it can be cost-effective for powering houses and businesses." He tells us that in the future most houses will have solar panels.

There are other problems with solar power. It needs a lot of space and, of course, it doesn't work at night.

WIND POWER

One afternoon I stood in a field in Denmark under a dark, cloudy sky. My solar panels produce very little energy in this weather. But above me a wind turbine was producing clean, renewable electricity. At the moment, wind power is the best of all the alternative energy sources. But again, there are problems. First, they are **ugly**; people don't like to see wind turbines in fields. And of course the wind doesn't blow all the time.

So, will our grandchildren get their energy from the sun, wind, or some other source? "We're going to need everything we can get from solar, everything we can get from wind," says Michael Pacheco, director of the National Bioenergy Center, part of the National Renewable Energy Laboratory (NREL) in Golden, Colorado. "And still the question is—can we get enough?"

Word Focus

alternative = something different *I don't like this idea. Is there an alternative?*
renewable = something you can use again and again
cost-effective = something that is cost-effective saves a lot of money
ugly = not beautiful

Writing

A. Work with a partner. Write statements about the future using the information in the box. Make your statements positive or negative.

people/live under the sea	**researchers/find alternative fuels**
people/enough food to eat	**people/travel to Mars**
scientists/find a cure for AIDS	**wars/end**

B. Use your ideas from exercise **A** to write a paragraph about the future.

In the next twenty-five years . . .

Goal 4 Discuss the future

Join two or three other students and discuss your ideas about the future.

E VIDEO JOURNAL *SOLAR COOKING*

Before You Watch

Discuss these questions with a partner.

1. What fuels can you use to cook food?
2. What fuel do you use to cook food?

▲ gas

▲ electricity

▲ firewood

▲ solar energy

▲ wind

While You Watch

A. Watch the video and match the people and their comments.

1. Eleanor Shimeall ___
2. Dr. Bob Metcalf ___
3. African woman ___

a. And the smoke from that fire—it burns their eyes and chokes their lungs.
b. I'm going to check on this chicken and rice and see how it's cooking. Ah, it's doing a good job.
c. We're all amazed that a cardboard box can cook.

B. Watch the video again. Check (✓) the correct box.

	Benefits of solar ovens	
	Health	Environmental
1. You don't have to cut down trees.	☐	☐
2. African women don't have to walk a long way to collect firewood.	☐	☐
3. There is no smoke.	☐	☐
4. Solar ovens can be used to make water clean.	☐	☐
5. Solar ovens don't cause pollution.	☐	☐

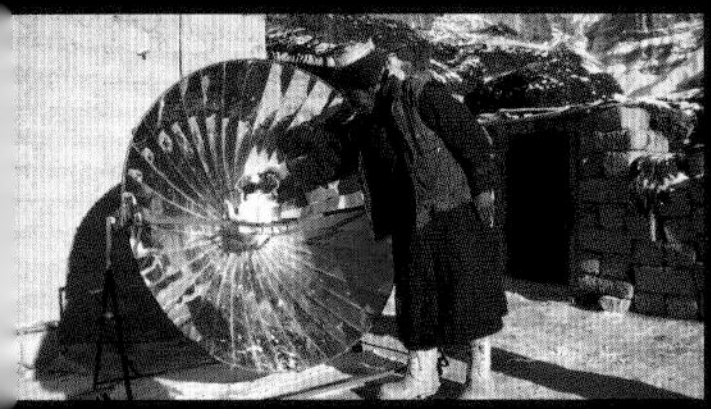

C. Watch again and answer the questions.

1. What can you cook in a solar oven? ______________________
2. What are the goals of Solar Cookers International? ______________
3. To what temperature must you heat water to make it safe to drink?

____

After You Watch

Work with a partner. Could you make a solar oven? Make a list of material you need to make a solar oven. Write instructions on how to make a solar oven. Use drawings if necessary.

▲ solar cooking

Communication

Role-play the following situation.

Student A

You are running a workshop in Africa. You have to explain the benefits of using solar ovens. Some of the participants have doubts.

Student B

You are a participant in the workshop. Your mother cooked with wood and you cook with wood. You have doubts about changing to something new. Express your doubts. Ask questions.

SHOPPING FOR

1. Where are these people from?

2. Which clothes do you like? Why?

UNIT GOALS

Make comparisons
Explain preferences
Talk about clothing materials
Understand and describe a process

CLOTHES

UNIT 9

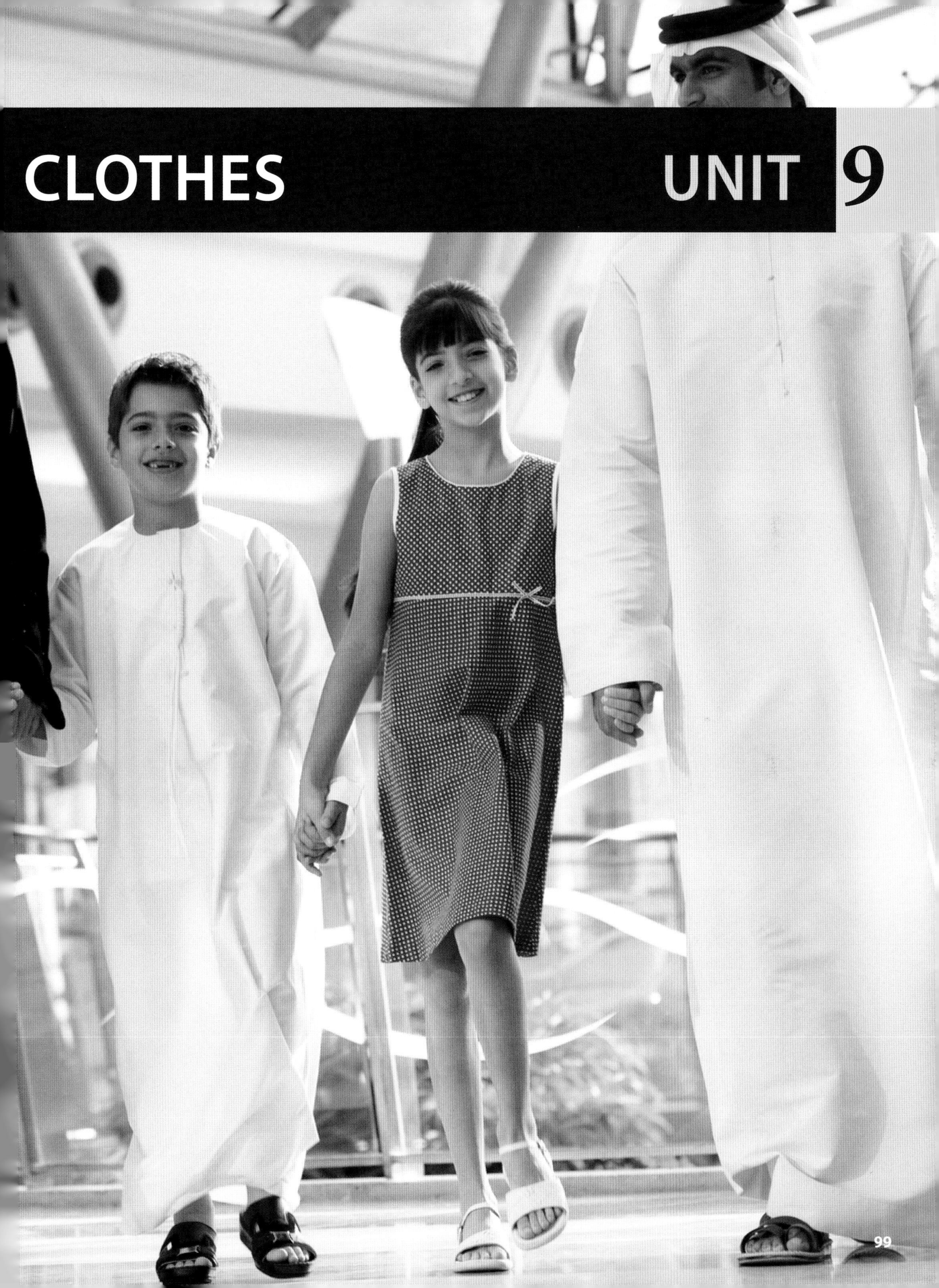

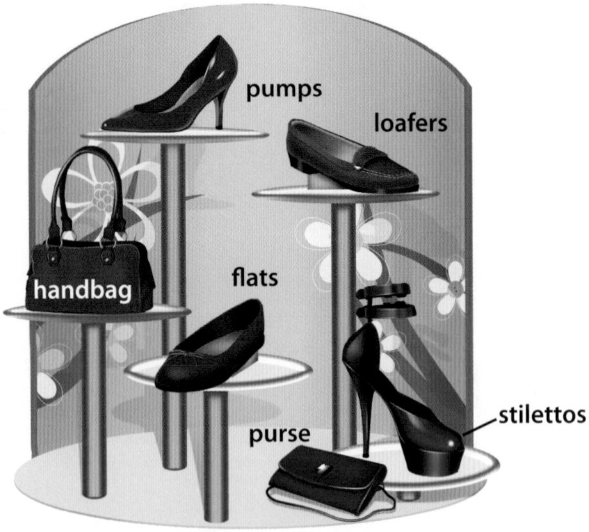

Vocabulary

A. Circle the word in each row that does not belong. Tell a partner why.

1. (dress)	pajamas	robe	nightgown
2. sweater	gloves	swimsuit	coat
3. shoes	socks	hat	loafers
4. jeans	T-shirt	suit	pumps
5. handbag	stilettos	pumps	loafers
6. stilettos	boots	slippers	coat

B. Underline the adjectives that describe clothes.

1. Fatima is wearing a thick, handmade sweater and she's warm.
2. Charles is wearing a poor quality, thin coat and he's cold.
3. John wore an expensive, formal business suit to the interview.
4. Andrew wore a cheap, casual jacket. Guess who got the job!
5. Aisha bought her daughter a soft, warm pair of pajamas.
6. Betty bought her child some poor quality, thin pajamas. Which child woke up at 3:00 a.m.?
7. Fiona went to the park wearing a modern pair of denim jeans and a pale green T-shirt.
8. Elena went wearing old-fashioned khaki pants and a sweatshirt. Guess who was hot!

C. Complete the sentences with the words that you underlined in exercise **B**.

1. It's going to be cold tomorrow. You should take a ________________ jacket.
2. You can't wear those ________________ jeans. You need to buy some modern ones.
3. ________________ clothes are always more expensive than machine-made clothes.
4. Looks are important, so I always wear a ________________ su when I meet clients.
5. This sweater is too light. Where is my ________________ one

D. Match the opposites.

1. formal ___	a. cool
2. old-fashioned ___	b. expensive
3. cheap ___	c. fashionable, modern
4. rough, hard ___	d. heavy
5. handmade ___	e. casual, informal
6. thick ___	f. machine made
7. warm ___	g. soft
8. light ___	h. thin

Grammar: Comparatives

Comparative forms of adjectives		
Adjectives with one syllable Add *-er*.	cheap	Machine-made sweaters are **cheaper than** handmade sweaters.
Adjectives that end in *-y* Change the *-y* to *i* and add *-er*.	pretty	This dress is **prettier than** that one.
Adjectives with two or more syllables Use *more* or *less* before the adjective.	beautiful	This flower is **more beautiful than** that one.
	expensive	These suits are **less expensive than** those.
Irregular comparatives	good	Shopping in a store is **better than** shopping online.
	bad	My grades are **worse than** yours.
*The comparative form is followed by *than*. *Use *much* to make a comparison stronger. *This coat is **much better than** the other one.*		

Complete the sentences. Use the comparative form of the word in parentheses.

1. I prefer the green handbag, but it is ______________ (expensive) than the blue purse.
2. These scarves are ______________ (nice) than those.
3. These shoes are ______________ (formal) than those.
4. The wool gloves are ______________ (soft) than the leather ones.
5. I think the blue slippers are ______________ (pretty) than the black ones.

Real Language

We can say *I don't know* or *I'm not sure* to show uncertainty.

Conversation

Track 2-12

A. Listen to the conversation. Danny and Elena are shopping. What is Elena looking for?

Danny: Look at these black shoes. They look nice.
Elena: I don't know. I need something more formal. They're for work.
Danny: What about these blue ones?
Elena: Mmm, I'm not sure. They're a little expensive.
Danny: Look! Here are some cheaper ones.
Elena: Yes, they're very nice. Oh, they're a size 8. Do they have them in a smaller size?
Danny: Yes, here we are.
Elena: Perfect.

B. Practice the conversation. Switch roles and practice it again.

Goal 1 Make comparisons

Compare your clothes with a partner's clothes.

I like your jeans. They're nicer than mine.

Listening

Track 2-13

A. Listen. What is the woman buying?

Track 2-13

B. Listen again and answer the questions.

1. How many pairs of shoes does the woman try on? ____________________
2. How much did the white shoes cost? ______________________________
3. How much did the black shoes cost? ______________________________
4. What size shoes does the woman wear? ____________________________
5. What color were the shoes that the woman bought? _________________

C. Match the questions and the answers.

1. Can I try them on? ____
2. Cash or charge? ____
3. How much are they? ____
4. What size are you? ____

a. They're $65.
b. I'm a 12.
c. Yes, the dressing rooms are over there.
d. I'll put it on my card.

Pronunciation: Rising and falling intonation

Track 2-14

A. Listen to the sentences. Write the arrows to show rising or falling intonation.

1. Which swimsuit is cheaper (↘)? The blue one (↗) or the red one (↘)?
2. Whose dress is prettier? Karen's or Mia's?
3. Which is easier? Shopping online or store shopping?
4. Which do you think is warmer? The sweater or the jacket?
5. Who is taller? Saeed or Haroun?

Track 2-14

B. Listen again. Repeat the sentences.

Communication

Discuss the questions with a partner. Make a list of your ideas.

1. What are the advantages and disadvantages of shopping online?
2. What are the advantages and disadvantages of shopping in a store?

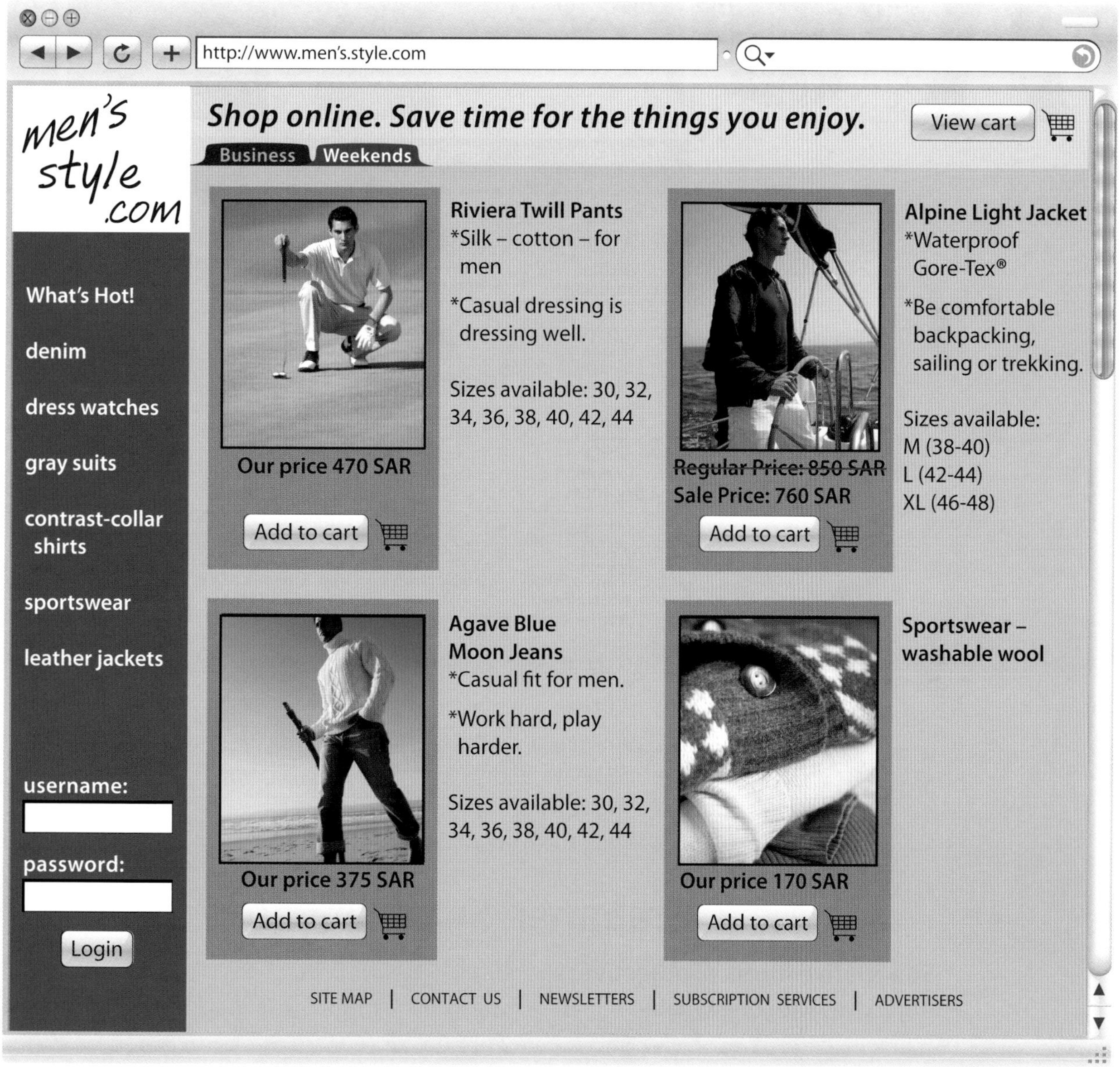

Goal 2 Explain preferences

What things do you prefer to buy online? What things do you prefer to buy in a store? Why? Share your ideas with a partner.

C GOAL 3 TALK ABOUT CLOTHING MATERIALS

Language Expansion: Clothing materials

A. Take turns describing the clothes in the pictures to a partner.

I really like that leather jacket.

100% Cotton Made in USA	100% Wool Made in Scotland	Man-made fiber Made in Taiwan	100% Leather Made in Argentina	Pure Silk Made in China
Machine Wash, WARM	Hand Wash	Machine Wash, HOT Permanent Press	Do Not Wash	Dry Clean
Bleach as Needed	Do Not Bleach	Bleach as Needed		Do Not Bleach
Tumble Dry, HIGH	Dry Flat	Tumble Dry, MEDIUM		Tumble Dry, MEDIUM
Iron, Steam, or Dry, with HIGH HEAT	Do Not Iron	Iron, Steam, or Dry, withLOW HEAT		Iron, Steam or Dry, with LOW HEAT

B. Read the different care instructions above. Circle **T** for *true* and **F** for *false*.

1. You can use bleach with cotton. T F
2. You can dry wool in a tumble drier. T F
3. You have to dry clean silk. T F
4. You can iron cotton. T F
5. You mustn't wash leather. T F

Grammar: Superlatives

Superlative forms of adjectives		
Adjectives with one syllable Add *-est.*	cheap	The cotton pajamas are **the cheapest**.
Adjectives that end in *-y* Change the *-y* to *i* and add *-est.*	pretty	This is **the prettiest** dress in the shop.
Adjectives with two or more syllables Use *most* or *least* before the adjective.	beautiful	These are **the most beautiful** shoes in the store.
	expensive	This suit is **the least expensive** one they have.
Irregular superlatives	good	Turner's is **the best** shoe store in town.
	bad	My English isn't good, but I don't have **the worst** grades in class.

*The superlative form is preceded by *the.*

A. Complete the sentences. Use the superlative form of the adjective in parentheses.

1. These are ____________________ (expensive) shoes in the store.
2. Which is ____________________ (warm) jacket? The red one, the brown one, or the blue one?
3. Granger's Discount Store has ____________________ (good) prices.
4. These are ____________________ (formal) shoes that we have.

B. Write sentences using the pairs of adjectives in the box.

cheap/expensive	**light/heavy**	**warm/cool**	**rough/smooth**

1. *Wool is usually more expensive than cotton, but silk is the most expensive material.*
2. *Wool is cheaper than silk, but usually cotton is the cheapest.*
3. ____
4. ____
5. ____
6. ____

Conversation

Track 2-15

A. Listen to the conversation. Why doesn't Steve like the leather jacket?

Steve: Excuse me, could you help me? I'm looking for a jacket.
Shop attendant: Certainly, sir. I have some over here.
Steve: Mmm, very nice. Which is the warmest?
Shop attendant: Well, these GORE-TEX® jackets are the warmest. They're waterproof and not too expensive
Steve: No, I don't really like man-made material.
Shop attendant: Well, we have some nice leather jackets.
Steve: No, I don't really like leather. It's very heavy, and I suppose they are the most expensive.
Shop attendant: Yes, I'm afraid so. The cheapest is $250.

B. Practice the conversation. Switch roles and practice it again.

C. Work with a partner to make a new conversation. This time try on something different.

Goal 3 Talk about clothing materials

Talk with a partner. Which is your favorite material? Why?

D GOAL 4 UNDERSTAND AND DESCRIBE A PROCESS

▲ Hubert de Givenchy, a French fashion designer, loves working with silk. "It is living. It moves," he says. "It immediately suggests the design of the dress."

Reading

A. Discuss these questions with a partner.

1. What do you know about silk?
2. How is silk made?

B. Answer the questions.

1. Which is the most expensive—cotton, wool, or silk? ______________
2. Which country is the biggest producer of silk? ______________
3. Why does Shen Congwen think that old silks are more beautiful than modern silks? ______________
4. Why do the workers put the cocoons into hot water? ______________
5. Do you agree that "A woman is more gentle when she wears a silk kimono"? Give your reasons. ______________

Silk—the Queen of Textiles

Cotton is cool; wool is warm. They're practical. But silk? Silk is soft, it is smooth, it is sophisticated—the queen of textiles. It is also possibly the most expensive material in the world, and indeed in ancient Rome it was more expensive than gold. But it is strong as well—a thread of silk is stronger than **steel**.

I wanted to discover more about this mysterious material, so I decided to go to China. China is where the secret of silk was discovered more than 4,000 years ago, and today it is still the biggest producer of silk in the world.

The first person I visited was Shen Congwen, advisor on ancient textiles to the Palace Museum in Beijing. He showed me some silk that workers found in a **tomb** in Jianglin, in Hubei Province. It was more than 2,000 years old but still beautiful. He told me that he thinks these old silks are more beautiful than modern silks. "In ancient times, weaving was done from the heart. In modern times, weaving is done for **commerce**."

So, how do you make silk? The first problem is that the silkworm only eats leaves from one tree—the mulberry tree. "It

▼ Silkworms feed on mulberry leaves.

▼ A silkworm spins a cocoon from silk thread.

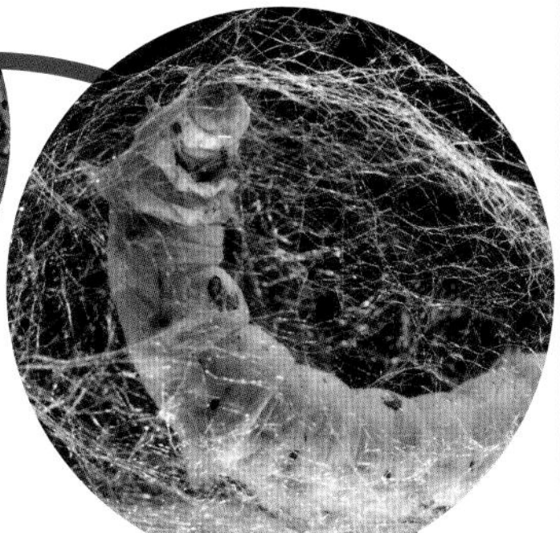

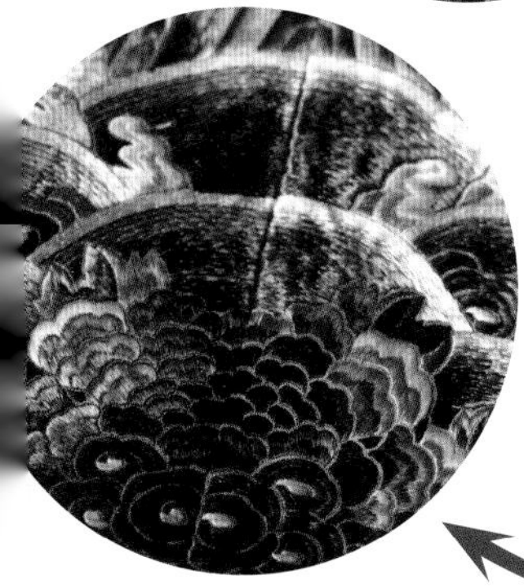

▲ A silk tapestry

▶ An artisan weaves silk cloth from threads on a loom.

is easier to prepare food for a human than a silkworm," says Toshio Ito, a Japanese silkworm physiologist. Silkworms only live for about 28 days, but in that time they increase in weight 10,000 times. At the end of their short lives, they **spin** a **cocoon**. In China, I watched workers collect the cocoons and kill the silkworms with steam or hot air. They then put the cocoons into hot water to make them softer. Next, they pulled the fibers from the cocoon and spun them to make silk thread. Finally, they wove the thread into cloth on machines called **looms**.

But why is silk so expensive? Well, it takes 110 cocoons to make a man's tie, 630 cocoons to make a blouse and 3,000 cocoons to make a heavy silk kimono. That's a lot of mulberry leaves and many hours of hard work. But many people believe its beauty is worth it. As Kokoh Moriguchi, a textile artist told me, "A woman is more gentle when she wears a silk kimono."

Word Focus

steel = a strong, hard metal
tomb = a place where dead people are buried
commerce = business, to make money

Writing

Write a paragraph about your favorite piece of clothing. Answer the questions.

- What is it made from?
- Where did you get it?
- When did you get it?
- How much did it cost?
- Why do you like it?

My favorite piece of clothing is a silk scarf. It was a present from my grandmother. She gave it to me when I was 10 years old. I don't know how much it cost but silk is very expensive. It is a beautiful deep red and it is very, very soft. I love it.

✓ Goal 4 Understand and describe a process

Work with a partner. Describe the process for making silk.

E VIDEO JOURNAL *TRADITIONAL SILK MAKING*

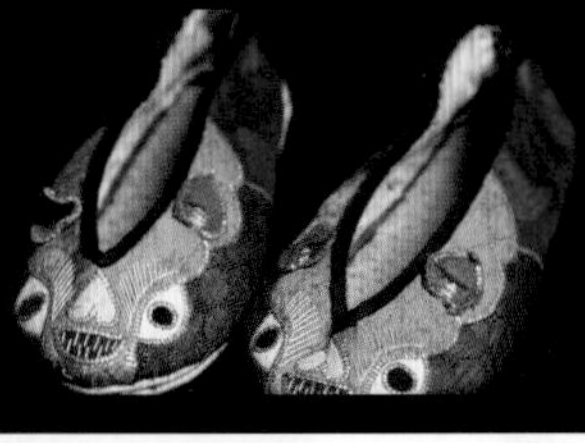

Before You Watch

A. Talk to a partner. Discuss how silk thread is different from wool, cotton, and synthetic threads.

B. Match the opposites.

1. noisy ___	a. different
2. same ___	b. quickly
3. modern ___	c. quiet
4. slowly ___	d. ancient
5. beautiful ___	e. ugly

C. Circle the words in exercise **B** that you think you will hear in the video. Watch the video and check your answers.

While You Watch

A. Watch the video and circle **T** for *true* and **F** for *false*

1. Florence is a modern city.	T	F
2. The factory manager is a man.	T	F
3. There are lots of women working in the factory.	T	F

B. Watch again. Circle the correct answer.

1. The Industrial Revolution, __________, and floods forced change.
   a. world wars
   b. the cold war
   c. world laws
2. The mechanical looms were made __________.
   a. in 1780
   b. in the 19th century
   c. 500 years ago
3. Other manufacturers threw away their old hand looms
   __________.
   a. after World War I
   b. 500 years ago
   c. after World War II

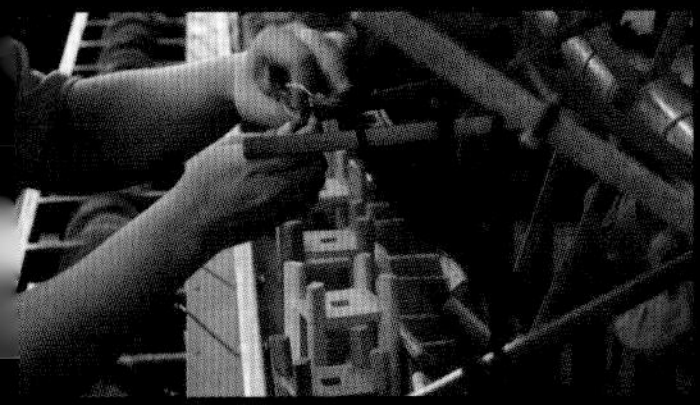

4. The silk produced on antique hand looms has ____________.
   a. 4,000 threads
   b. 12,000 threads
   c. 3,000 threads
5. Every damask and brocade is ____________.
   a. man-made
   b. handmade
   c. custom-made

▲ loom

After You Watch

Discuss these questions with a partner.

1. Why do you think Stefano Benelli is the only man in the video?
2. Are men better at some jobs than women? Why?
3. At which jobs are women better than men? Why?

▲ brocade

Communication

Role-play the following situation.

Student A
You are a sales assistant in a textile shop. Try to sell the handmade silk.

Handmade silk brocade	Machine-made silk	Artificial silk (acetate)
Price: $55-$100 per meter	**Price:** $25-$35 per meter	**Price:** $15-$25 per meter

Student B
You are a customer. You want 5 meters of cloth for some curtains. You can spend about $200.

LIFESTYLES

1. Which of these photos show a healthy lifestyle?
2. How is your lifestyle? Can you improve it?

UNIT GOALS

Give advice on healthy habits
Suggest ways to improve bad habits
Ask about lifestyles
Evaluate your lifestyle

UNIT 10

Vocabulary

Alicia has a **healthy** lifestyle. She's in **good shape** because she **works out** in the gym every day. She eats healthy food, like fruit and fresh vegetables.

Alan doesn't have a good **lifestyle**. He's **unfit** because he never does any exercise. He eats too much **junk food** so he's overweight. He's in **bad shape**.

A. Complete the sentences with the words in **blue**.

1. I need to exercise more. I'm in ____________________.
2. Helen doesn't have a ____________________ diet. She eats a lot of junk food.
3. I have a good ____________________. I don't smoke, I exercise regularly, and I don't eat ____________________.
4. I need to exercise more. I'm ____________________, and I'm overweight.
5. Jane is looking great! She ____________________ and eats healthy food like whole grain bread and lots of fruit. Soon she'll be in ____________________.

B. Write the activities in the correct column.

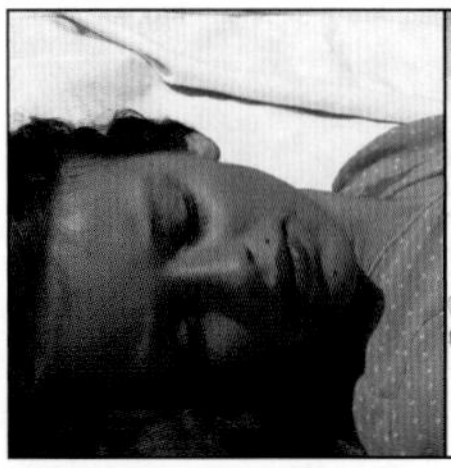

▲ sunbathing

▲ smoking

▲ watching lots of TV

▲ cycling

▲ getting eight hours sleep every night

▲ drinking lots of water

▲ eating a balanced diet

▲ eating lots of sugar

Healthy	Unhealthy

Grammar: Modals—*could, ought to, should, must, have to*

Could, ought to, should, must, have to		
Make suggestions	**Give advice**	**Express obligation**
You **could** stop smoking.	You **should/ought to** stop smoking.	You **must/have to** stop smoking.
! gentle	!! strong	!!! very strong

A. Take turns. Make suggestions, give advice, or express obligations. Use the activities on page 112.

B. Give advice for the following situations.

1. Tell your sister to stop smoking. !!!
   ____
2. Tell to your father go on a diet. !!
   ____
3. Tell your friend to stop watching so much television. !
   ____

Conversation

Track 2-16

A. Listen to the conversation. Why does Mia want to lose weight?

Mia: I need to lose some weight. My clothes don't fit anymore. What should I do?
Alex: Well, instead of watching TV all day, you could do more exercise.
Mia: Like what?
Alex: Like cycling, or you could work out at the gym.
Mia: I don't have time. I'm too busy.
Alex: OK, then you could change your diet. Eat something healthier, like fruit.
Mia: You mean no more burgers! Oh no!
Alex: OK. Buy some bigger clothes then.

Real Language

We use *like what* to ask for an example. We can use *like* to give an example.

B. Practice the conversation with a partner. Switch roles and practice it again.

✓ Goal 1 Give advice on healthy habits

Take turns. Give a partner suggestions on how to improve his or her health.

Listening

Track 2-17

A. Look at the pictures. Who do you think has an unhealthy lifestyle? Listen and check your prediction.

▲ Ben

▲ Maggie

▲ Anita

Track 2-17

B. Listen again and answer the questions.

1. Does Ben exercise every day? ______________________________
2. Does Ben smoke? ______________________________
3. What exercise does Maggie do? ______________________________
4. Name two things that Maggie has for breakfast. ______________________________
5. Where does Anita get her vegetables? ______________________________
6. What is Anita's one bad habit? ______________________________

C. Work with a partner. What advice would you give to Ben, Maggie, and Anita on how to improve their lifestyles?

Pronunciation: *Should, shouldn't*

Track 2-18

A. Listen to the sentences. Notice the difference between *should* and *shouldn't*.

I **should** get more sleep.
They **shouldn't** eat junk food.

Track 2-19

B. Listen and circle the word you hear.

1. You should/shouldn't go to bed at one o'clock every night.
2. You should/shouldn't drink less coffee.
3. Zeta should/shouldn't lose some weight.
4. They should/shouldn't watch so much TV.

Track 2-19

C. Listen again and repeat the sentences.

Communication

Take turns. Talk about these bad habits and give advice.

She's worried that she is gaining weight.

What advice are you going to give her?

Well, she should stop eating junk food. She should . . .

Goal 2 Suggest ways to improve bad habits

Ask two partners about their bad habits. Give them advice.

▲ mouth-watering fruit

▲ homemade pie

Language Expansion: Compound adjectives

A. Match the compound adjectives to their meanings.

1. mouth-watering ___
2. homemade ___
3. heart-warming ___
4. lifelong ___
5. stress-free ___
6. homegrown ___
7. overworked ___
8. low-calorie ___

a. works too much
b. delicious
c. without worries or problems
d. not high in calories
e. makes you happy
f. produced in your own garden
g. all your life
h. not made in a factory

B. Complete the sentences. Use the adjectives from exercise **A**.

1. Kevin and I went to kindergarten together. We are __________________ friends.
2. When I was a child, my father had a vegetable garden, so we ate lots of __________________ fruit and vegetables.
3. I have to work long hours and I'm always tired. I think I am __________________.
4. My grandmother makes the best __________________ chicken soup in the world! It's absolutely __________________.

Grammar: Questions with *how*

How much exercise do you do?
How many cigarettes do you smoke?
How old is your father?
How long did your grandfather live?
How often do you go to the gym?

*We use **how much** to ask about the quantity of non-countable nouns.
*We use **how many** to ask about the quantity of countable nouns.
*We use **how old** to ask about age.
*We use **how long** to ask about length or a period of time.
*We use **how often** to ask about frequency.

A. Match the questions and the answers.

1. How often does Ian go swimming? ___
2. How old is Akuru's grandmother? ___
3. How much junk food do you eat? ___
4. How long do you think you will live? ___
5. How many cigarettes does Mario smoke a day? ___

a. She's about 95.
b. Until I'm 80.
c. About 15.
d. Not much.
e. Once a week.

B. Write the questions.

Questions	Answers
1. ______________________	We go to the gym three times a week.
2. ______________________	I am 27 years old.
3. ______________________	I think it will take about two hours.
4. ______________________	I weigh 168 lbs.
5. ______________________	We will need another 12 chairs.

Conversation

Track 2-20

A. Listen to the conversation. What's the problem with Mr. Lopez?

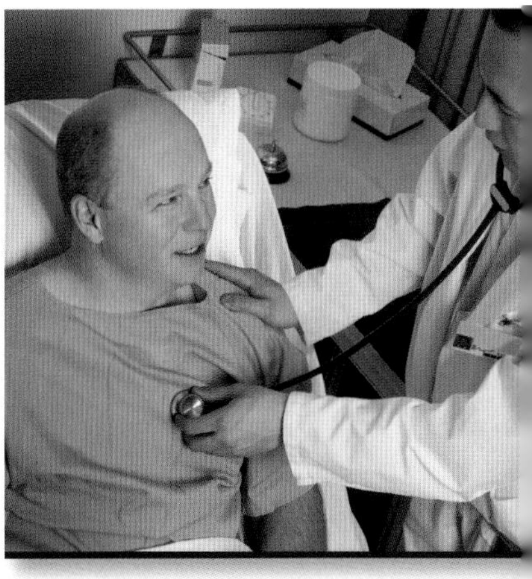

Doctor: Good morning, Mr. Lopez. How can I help you?
Mr. Lopez: Yes, doctor. <u>I'm always tired but when I go to bed I can't sleep</u>.
Doctor: OK, how long have you had this problem?
Mr. Lopez: Since I started my new job.
Doctor: What is your job?
Mr. Lopez: I'm in advertising.
Doctor: How many hours do you work?
Mr. Lopez: I work about 80 hours a week.
Doctor: 80 hours! That's a lot. And how much exercise do you do?
Mr. Lopez: Not much. I don't have the time.
Doctor: OK, it seems to me that you are overworked. You need to work less and find time to do more exercise. Maybe you should look for a more stress-free job.

B. Practice the conversation with a partner. Switch roles and practice it again.

C. Change the underlined problem and practice a new conversation.

Goal 3 Ask about lifestyles

Ask a partner about his or her lifestyle.

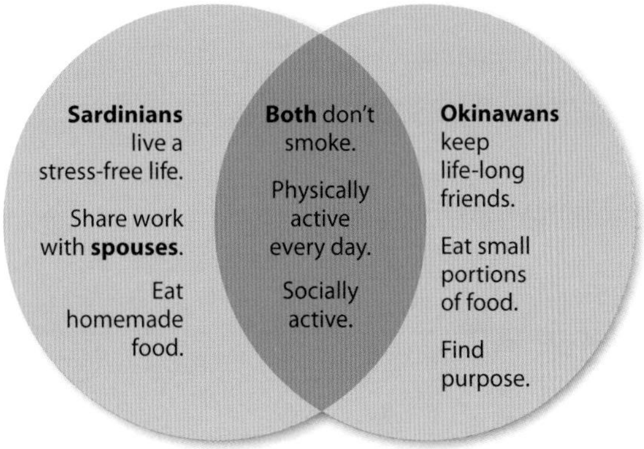

▲ Lifestyles that make you live longer

Reading

A. Discuss the following questions with a partner.

1. Do you want to live to be 100 years old?
2. What can you do to live to be 100 years old?

Word Focus

spouse = wife or husband
genes = part of the body that determines physical characteristiscs
run away = to leave
perfume = liquid that smells good
joke = to say something that is not serious
prevent = to avoid

The Secrets of Long Life

A long, healthy life is no accident. It begins with good **genes**, but it also depends on good habits. If you have a healthy lifestyle, experts say, you may live up to 10 years longer. So what is the secret of a long life?

I visited places in the world where many people live to be 100 years old—including Sardinia in Italy and Okinawa in Japan. Sardinians and Okinawans live longer, suffer from fewer illnesses, and enjoy long, healthy lives.

SARDINIANS

First I went to Sardinia, where many people, especially men, live longer than in other parts of the world. Generally, women live longer than men. In fact, in America, there are four times as many 100-year-old women as men. However, in Sardinia an equal number of men and women reach 100.

The reason is possibly that the men have a stress-free life working in the hills, and the women look after the house and the family money. "I do the work," says Tonino. "My wife does the worrying."

▲ Tonino's family's diet is another factor. They eat lots of home-grown fruits and vegetables such as zucchini, eggplant, tomatoes, and fava beans that may reduce the risk of heart disease and colon cancer.

OKINAWANS

Since I last visited Ushi five years ago, she's taken a new job, tried to **run away** from home, and started wearing **perfume**. Normal for a young woman, perhaps, but Ushi is 103. When I ask about the perfume, she **jokes**, then puts a hand over her mouth and gives a long heart-warming laugh.

"Okinawans have one-fifth the heart disease, one-fourth the breast and prostate cancer, and one-third less mental health problems than Americans," says Craig Willcox of the Okinawa Centenarian Study. What's the key to their success? "Ikigai certainly helps," Willcox says. The word translates to "reason for living," and it may help to prevent stress and diseases such as high blood pressure.

Okinawans have a low-calorie diet. "A full plate of Okinawan vegetables, tofu, miso soup, and a little fish or meat contains fewer calories than a small burger," says Makoto Suzuki of the Okinawa Centenarian Study. "And it will have many more healthy nutrients."

▲ When she's not watching sumo wrestling on TV, Yasu Itoman, 100, gets her own exercise by growing onions, tomatoes, carrots, and other herbs and vegetables in her garden. Her homegrown vegetables give her natural antioxidants that may help **prevent** cancer.

B. Answer the questions

1. A long, healthy life depends on mainly two things. What are they? ________
2. Why do men live longer in Sardinia than in the United States? ________
3. How old was Ushi the last time the writer visited her? ________
4. How often should you exercise? ________
5. What are the advantages of growing your own vegetables? ________

Writing

Write a paragraph about your own lifestyle. Answer the questions.

1. Do you lead a healthy lifestyle?
2. How often do you exercise?
3. What sort of food do you eat?
4. Do you smoke?
5. Do you get enough sleep?
6. How can you improve your lifestyle?

Goal 4 **Evaluate your lifestyle**

Take turns. Discuss with a partner the good habits and the bad habits in your lifestyles. Give each other advice.

E VIDEO JOURNAL *THE SCIENCE OF STRESS*

Before You Watch

A. Look at the photos. Which of these cause stress?

B. Match the words and the definitions.

1. hormones ___
2. physical stress ___
3. mental stress ___

a. stress on your body, like running
b. stress on your mind, like too much work
c. chemical that your body produces

While You Watch

A. Watch the video. Circle **T** for *true* and **F** for *false*.

1. There are two types of stress: physical and mental. T F
2. Stress produces hormones. T F
3. When you exercise, you don't burn all the hormones. T F
4. Long-term hormones can cause problems. T F

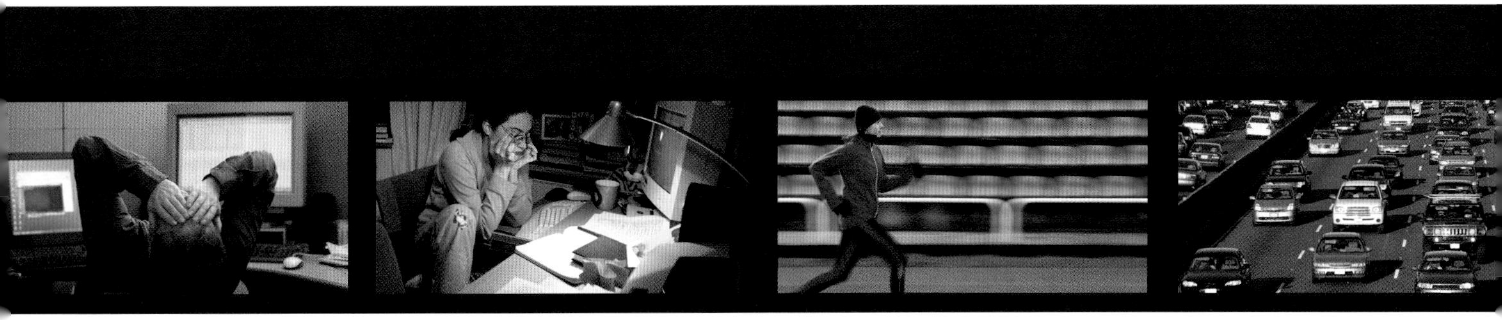

B. Write the following words and expressions in the **stress** flowchart.

burns	**No**	**too much work**	**hormones**

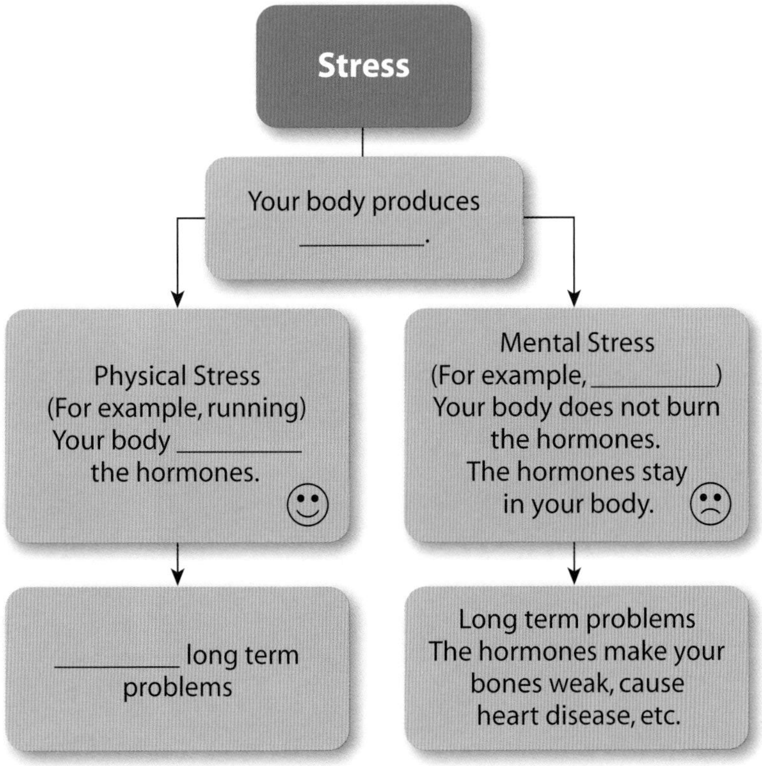

Word Focus

If you feel under **stress**, you feel worried and tense because of difficulties in your life.

After You Watch

Discuss the questions with a partner.

1. What did you learn from this video?
2. Will it change your lifestyle?

Communication

Work in a group of three or four students. You have been assigned to design your school's or office's Antistress Campaign. Make a list of four things you will do.

ACHIEVEMENTS

1. What have these people achieved?
2. What have you achieved in your life so far?

UNIT GOALS

Talk about today's chores
Interview for a job
Talk about lifetime achievements
Discuss scientific achievements

UNIT 11

Vocabulary

A. Label the pictures with phrases from the box.

pay the bills
buy the groceries
sweep the floor
cut the grass
walk the dog
vacuum
iron the clothes
put away the clothes

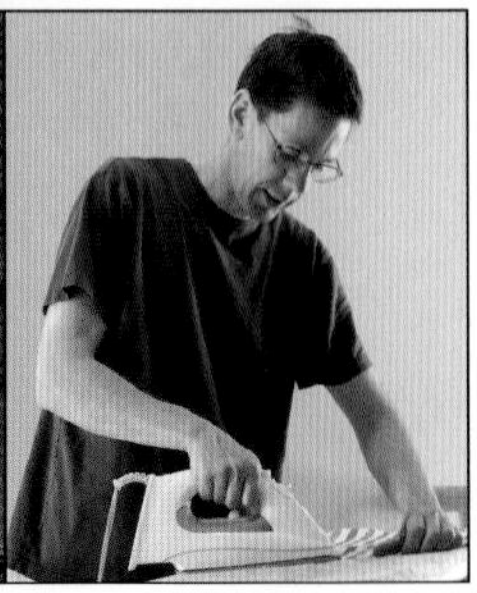

1. ________ 2. ________ 3. ________ 4. ________

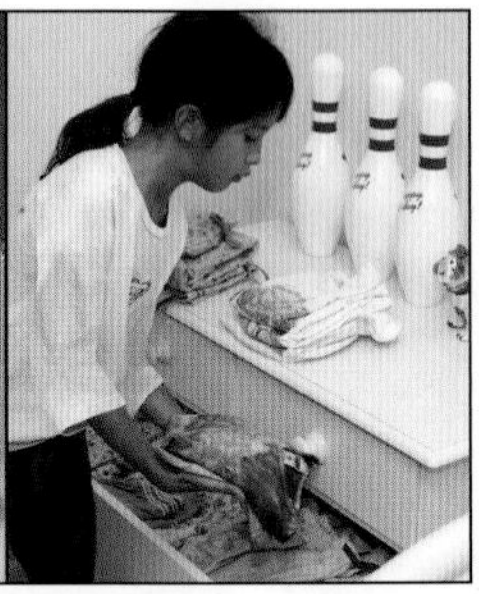

5. ________ 6. ________ 7. ________ 8. ________

B. Write the activities from exercise **A** in the correct column.

Easy chores	Difficult chores
walk the dog	

Word Focus

chore = A *chore* is a task that you must do, but that you find boring or unpleasant.

C. Discuss with a partner. In your family, who does the household chores?

Grammar: Present perfect tense

Present perfect tense	
Statement	He **has ironed** the clothes.
Negative	I **haven't cooked** lunch yet.
Yes/no questions	**Have you finished** your homework?
Short answers	Yes, I **have**. No, I **haven't.**
Information questions	What **have you done** today?

*The present perfect tense is formed with the verb *has/have* + the past participle of the verb.
*We use the present perfect tense to talk about an action that has just been completed or to talk about an action that happened in the past but will happen again in the present or future.

*Some verbs have regular past participles. They end in *-ed*.		*Some verbs have irregular past participles.	
pass – passed	graduate – graduated	have – had	take – took
clean – cleaned	travel – traveled	go – gone	pay – paid
iron – ironed	visit– visited	be – been	put – put

A. Match the past participle forms to the verbs.

1. eaten ___	a. meet
2. drunk ___	b. tell
3. swept ___	c. eat
4. met ___	d. say
5. said ___	e. speak
6. spoken ___	f. drink
7. told ___	g. win
8. won ___	h. sweep
9. bought ___	i. read
10. read ___	j. buy

B. Complete the sentences with the present perfect tense. Use the words in parentheses.

1. Alan ________________ (wash) the car.
2. ________________ (you, buy) the groceries?
3. I ________________ (not, put away) the clothes.
4. ________________ (Peter, sweep) the floor?
5. They ________________ (not, pay) their telephone bill.

Real Language

We use *of course* to show something is obvious.

Conversation

Track 2-21

A. Read the note and listen to the conversation. Has Lynn done her chores?

Mom: Hi, honey, I'm home.
Lynn: Hi, Mom.
Mom: Have you walked the dog?
Lynn: Yes, Mom, of course I've walked the dog. And I've vacuumed the living room.
Mom: And have you done your homework?
Lynn: Mom! I've been busy walking the dog and vacuuming. I haven't had time.
Mom: Sorry, honey. It's just I've had a long day myself.

Honey, will you please do these things before I come home?
-vacuum the living room
-walk the dog

Thanks,
Mom

B. Practice the conversation with a partner. Switch roles and practice it again.

C. Write another chore list and practice the conversation again.

Goal 1 **Talk about today's chores**

Talk to a partner about the chores you have done today.

Listening

Track 2-22

A. Read the ad. Listen to Richard and Erin at the interview. Decide who should get the job. Give your reasons.

NEEDED URGENTLY!

TOUR GUIDE
Bermuda

Smart appearance. Good interpersonal skills. Experience an advantage. Driver's license essential. Call 2356 9845.

▲ Erin

▲ Richard

Track 2-22

B. The interviewer asked the following questions. Complete the questions. Listen again to check your answers.

1. Have you ______________ from college?
2. Have you ever ______________ as a tour guide?
3. Who is the most interesting person you have ever ______________?
4. Have you ______________ your driving test?

C. Answer the questions.

1. Has Richard ever traveled abroad? ______________
2. How many countries has Erin visited? ______________
3. Who is the most interesting person Erin has met? ______________
4. Has Richard passed his driving test? ______________
5. Has Erin graduated from college? ______________

Pronunciation: Reduced form of *have*

Track 2-23

A. Listen to the examples. Notice the pronunciation of the reduced forms.

Full form	Reduced form
I have	I've
have you	/'hav-yə/
you have	you've
has he	/'ha-zē/
she has	she's

Track 2-24

B. Listen to the sentences. Check the correct column.

	Full form	Reduced form
1. **Has she** left?		
2. **Have you** finished?		
3. **Has he** read this book?		
4. **Have you** done your homework?		
5. **I have** never been to the United States.		

Track 2-24

C. Listen again. Repeat the sentences.

Communication

Interview a partner for the following jobs.

WANTED!

Handyman for Kindergarten

Small kindergarten needs a person to help with maintenance—plumbing, carpentry, fixing our vehicles, etc. No experience with children necessary but must enjoy being around kids. Any age. DHS 75 per hour.

SALES ASSISTANT

Fashionable clothes shop is looking for a SALES ASSISTANT 18-30 years old, 2 p.m. to 10 p.m. Experience an advantage. Must have an interest in clothes and fashion. Salary negotiable.

Goal 2 Interview for a job

Think of another job. What's required? Write notes. Interview a partner.

Language Expansion: Lifetime achievements

A. Label the pictures with phrases from the box.

graduate from high school/ college	**travel abroad**	**pass your driving test**	**run a marathon**
get promotion	**buy your own car**	**buy a house**	**get a credit card**

1. ________ 2. ________ 3. ________ 4. ________

5. ________ 6. ________ 7. ________ 8. ________

B. Check the achievements in exercise **A** that you have done.

C. Take turns. Ask a partner what he or she has achieved.

Have you graduated from college?

Grammar: Present perfect tense vs. simple past tense

Present perfect tense vs. simple past tense	
The present perfect tense is used to show an action that happened at any time in the past. *Alan **has been** to many countries.*	The simple past tense is used to show an action that happened at a specific time in the past. *He **went** to France last year.*

*We often use time expressions with the simple past tense.
*We use expressions like *just, never, ever* with the present perfect tense.
*Have you **ever** been to another country?*
*Alan has **just** returned from France.*
*I have **never** been there.*

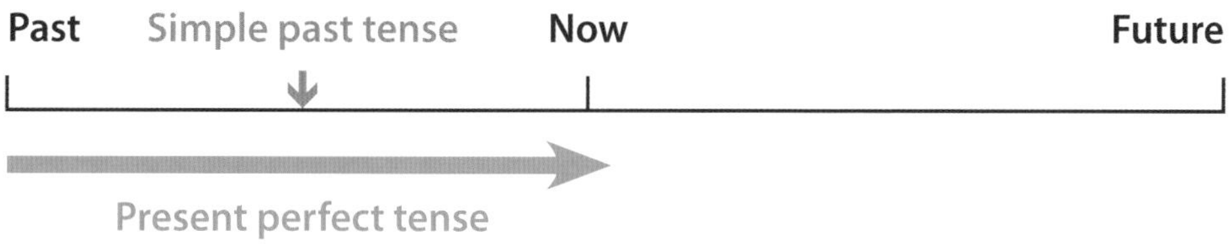

A. Complete the sentences with the correct form of the verb in parentheses.

1. Last summer, we ______________ (go) to the Maldives.
2. I ______________ (live) in the same house all my life.
3. John ______________ (never travel) abroad.
4. Italy ______________ (win) the World Cup in 2006.
5. Brazil ______________ (win) the World Cup five times.

B. Complete the conversations with the correct form of the verb in parentheses.

1. A: ______________ (you pass) your driving test?
   B: Yes. I ______________ (take) it in January and I ______________ (pass) the first time.
2. A: ______________ (you be) to Europe?
   B: Yes, I have. I ______________ (go) to Germany last year.

Conversation

Track 2-25

A. Listen to the conversation. Who has started his own business?

Simon: Hi, Pete. I haven't seen you for a long time. What's new?
Pete: Lots! I quit my job with CompuSoft and I've started my own computer business.
Simon: Congratulations! When did you open the business?
Pete: Eight months ago and it's going well.
Simon: Great.
Pete: And what about you?
Simon: Things haven't changed much. I'm still working at the bank. But I've bought a new house. It's on 5th and Main.
Pete: Wow! Nice neighborhood.
Simon: Yeah. You should come round and visit some time.
Pete: Will do. When I have some time.

B. Practice the conversation with a partner. Switch roles and practice it again.

C. Practice the conversation again. Change the underlined words.

Goal 3 **Talk about lifetime achievements**

Talk to a partner about your lifetime achievements.

Reading

A. Are there other planets outside the solar system? Read and check your answer.

▲ In 1996 astronomers discovered a planet orbiting the star Upsilon Andromedae. Recently they have found two more planets **orbiting** Upsilon Andromedae. This is the first evidence of a **solar system** beyond ours.

Word Focus

orbit = to go round and round a planet, moon, or star.
solar system = the sun and all the planets

Uncovering the Mysteries of the Universe

▲ Gary Puniwai is an observing assistant in the Keck Observatory control rooms on Mauna Kea, Hawaii.

GARY PUNIWAI sits at the controls of the Keck 1 telescope, the world's most powerful telescope on the summit of the highest peak in the Pacific. The telescope focuses on objects in space more than 10 billion years old.

Since people started looking at stars we have achieved a lot. The ancient Egyptians believed that the stars were very near—almost close enough to touch. Just a few hundred years ago, in the 16th and 17th centuries, most Europeans thought that the earth was the center of the universe and that the sun revolved around the earth. But modern science has expanded our understanding, and we know the earth is a small planet that goes around an ordinary star in the Milky Way Galaxy. We also know that there are more than 100 billion galaxies in the universe. We live on a small planet in a very large universe.

But there are many questions we haven't answered yet. Scientists have discovered that there are other planets in the universe. However, all the planets that they have found are much bigger than the earth—about the size of Jupiter—and they probably don't have life on them. But who knows?

Also we have discovered that the universe contains something called Dark Matter. We know it is there, but we can't see it and there is a lot of it. Some scientists say that as much as 70 percent of the universe is made from this Dark Matter. They have looked high and low for the missing matter, but they have not found it.

Science has achieved a lot, but there are still some very big questions we need to answer. Or will science reach some limit like the Pillars of Hercules, the classical symbol for what lies at the edge of what we know? On these pillars, according to legend, was written in Latin: "*Ne plus ultra*"—No further. Are there some things we will never understand?

B. Answer the questions.

1. What is Gary Puniwai's job? ______________________
2. Are there other planets outside our solar system? ______________________
3. Why is Dark Matter difficult to find? ______________________
4. What have we learned since people started looking at stars? ______________________
5. Do you think there are some things that we will never understand? Give your reasons. ______________________

Writing

Gary is writing to a friend. Answer the email.

Hi Ana

How's life? I haven't heard from you for a long time. What's new?
I've changed jobs three times since we last met. I'm now a technician at the Keck telescopes. I haven't been here long, but I like it. And guess what? I've started an online course in physics. Yes, I'm going to be a scientist.

Anyway, what have you done since I saw you last? Let me know.

Gary

Goal 4 **Discuss scientific achievements**

Talk to a partner about other scientific achievements.

E VIDEO JOURNAL *SPACEWALK*

Before You Watch

A. Look at the photos. What are the astronauts doing? Which activity do you think is the most dangerous. Why?

B. Read the summary of the video and fill in the blanks with words from the box. Then watch the video and check your answers.

weightless	**survive**	**underwater**	**oxygen**	**solar panels**

Video summary

Outside the earth's atmosphere, in space, there is no ____________________. It is impossible to breathe. Sometimes astronauts have to make a spacewalk outside the spacecraft. In order to ____________________, astronauts wear special space suits. They do jobs like repair ____________________. But it is difficult and dangerous work.

They prepare for their spacewalks ____________________ in special tanks. It is like being ____________________ in space but much safer.

While You Watch

A. Watch the video and complete the chart.

On earth	In space
The atmosphere protects us from dangerous radiation.	There is no atmosphere to protect the astronauts from dangerous radiation.
There is oxygen to breathe.	
Temperatures range from –50°C to 50°C.	
Gravity keeps us on the ground.	

B. Watch the video again and circle **T** for *true* or **F** for *false*.

1. It is always very cold in space. T F
2. Space suits are filled with oxygen. T F
3. The first person to walk in space was Edward White. T F
4. Astronauts fixed the solar panels on the Hubble Space Telescope. T F
5. Astronauts practice spacewalking in special tanks. T F

After You Watch

Man's scientific achievements are expensive. The National Aeronautics and Space Administration (NASA) spent $17 billion in 2008. The Large Hadron Collider (a gigantic scientific instrument), which opened in 2008, cost $4.6 billion. Discuss this with a partner. Why do governments spend a lot of money on big science projects?

Communication

Discuss with a partner other ways you could spend NASA's budget (money) to help people. Make a list of specific things you can do. Be prepared to share your list and the reasons for your choices with the class.

CONSEQUENCES

1. What is happening in each picture?
2. What are the possible results, effects, or consequences of these actions?

UNIT GOALS

Talk about managing your money
Make choices on how to spend your money
Talk about how our actions can have positive consequences
Discuss ways to prevent habitat destruction

UNIT 12

A GOAL 1 TALK ABOUT MANAGING YOUR MONEY

Vocabulary

A. Read the article from a student magazine.

STUDENT LIFE

MANAGE YOUR MONEY

Congratulations! You have received your first student loan. How are you going to spend it? Are you going to go out and buy that new cell phone or those cool sneakers? Well, don't!

Before you spend a penny, you have to make a **budget** and plan your spending. First write down your **income**—how much money you receive. Then calculate your **expenses** (rent, transportation, food). If your expenses are lower than your income, you are on the right road! Now you know how much money you have left to spend each month. But don't **overspend** or you will have to **borrow** money. Borrowing money from the bank is expensive. Interest rates are high. Always check to see if a friend or family member can **lend** you the money.

You also have to think about the long term. How are you going to pay for that spring break at the beach, or buy your family presents? You will have to **save** some money every month. So, that new cell phone can wait. Manage your money and maybe you'll be able to take that spring break at the beach–in Mexico!

21 November 2008

Word Focus

student loan = money that the government lends to students at a very low interest rate

B. Write the words in **blue** next to the correct meanings.

1. the amount of money you spend ______________
2. to ask someone to give you money ______________
3. the amount of money you receive ______________
4. to spend too much money ______________
5. a spending plan ______________
6. to give someone money ______________
7. to put money in the bank for the future ______________

Grammar: Real conditionals (or first conditional)

If **clause (simple present tense)**	**Result clause (future tense)**
If I **buy** an MP3,	I **will** not **have** enough money to pay the rent.
If they **borrow** some money,	they **will be able to** buy a new house.

*We use real conditional sentences to express possible consequences of choices we make.
*When the *if* clause comes first, there is a comma between the *if* clause and the result clause.

A. Match the *if* clauses to the correct result clauses.

1. If you borrow money from the bank, ____.
2. If you save some money every month, ____.
3. If you lend money to your sister, ____.
4. If your expenses are bigger than your income, ____.
5. If we eat in, ____.

a. she won't return the money until the end of the month
b. you won't have enough money to take a vacation
c. we will have enough money to go to the theater
d. the interest rates will be high
e. you will have enough money to buy a new computer

B. Unscramble the words to write conditional sentences. Don't forget the punctuation.

1. a bigger car / some money / we borrow / If / we can buy
   If we borrow some money, we can buy a bigger car.
2. a new job / more money / I will have / I get / If
   ____
3. on vacation / we overspend / If / to go / we won't be able
   ____
4. I won't have to / I / use my credit card / If / borrow money
   ____
5. our car / sell / we will be able to rent / If we / a bigger apartment
   ____

Conversation

Track 2-26

A. Listen to the conversation. What choice does Jim have to make?

Jim: I don't know what to do. I want to take a vacation and I also want to buy a new camera.

Dave: I see. If you buy the camera, you won't have enough money for the vacation. Is that it?

Jim: You got it.

Dave: So, just take the vacation. Don't buy the camera.

Jim: But if I don't buy the camera, I won't be able to take any vacation photos.

Dave: OK, just buy the camera.

Jim: But if I buy the camera, I won't be able to take the vacation and I won't need a camera.

Dave: Hmm . . . you have a problem

B. Practice the conversation with a partner. Switch roles and practice it again.

Goal 1 Talk about managing your money

Work with a partner. Discuss how you manage your money.

Listening

Track 2-27

A. Listen to the conversation. Circle the correct answer.

The travel agent is in ____.

a. London
b. Paris
c. New York

Track 2-27

B. Listen again and answer the questions.

1. Is this the first time that the woman has visited England? ____________
2. Why doesn't she want to take the plane? ____________
3. Why doesn't she want to rent a car? ____________
4. How long does it take to go from Paris to London by train? ____________
5. How much does the train ticket cost? ____________

Pronunciation: Intonation

Track 2-28

A. Listen to the sentences. Write the arrows to show rise or fall.

↗ ↘

1. If I buy a car, I won't be able to pay the rent.
2. If you take the bus, it will be cheaper.
3. If we borrow some money, we will repay it in a month.
4. If Sara leaves now, she will catch the seven o'clock train.
5. If we take the plane, it will be quicker.

Track 2-28

B. Listen again and repeat the sentences.

Communication

Work with a partner. Plan a six-day visit to California. Each of you has $200 to spend on transportation.You will arrive in Los Angeles. Your airport transfers are paid for. You would like to visit Yosemite, Sea World in San Diego, and San Francisco.

	San Diego	San Francisco	Merced (for Yosemite)
Los Angeles	❖$30, 4 hours ♦ $70, 3 hours ⇧$120, 1 hour	❖$50, 6 hours ♦ $60, 8 hours (3 changes) ⇧$120, 1½ hours	❖$70, 7 hours ♦ No service ⇧ No service
San Diego		❖$128 return, 12 hours ♦ No service ⇧ $250, 1½ hours	❖$82, 10 hours ♦ No service ⇧No service
San Francisco			❖$62, 4 hours ♦ $53, 3 hours ⇧No service

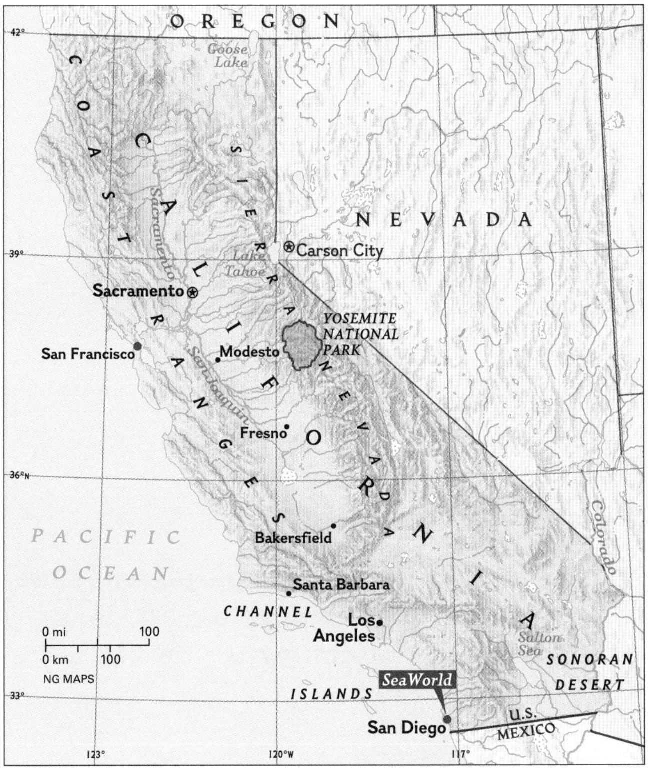

	Itinerary	Transport	Transport costs
Day 1			
Day 2			
Day 3			
Day 4			
Day 5			
Day 6			

Goal 2 **Make choices on how to spend your money**

Join another pair of students and explain to them how you decided to spend your transportation money.

C GOAL 3 TALK ABOUT HOW OUR ACTIONS CAN HAVE POSITIVE

Language Expansion: Animal habitats

A. Take turns. Make statements about animals and their habitats.

▲ desert

▲ mountains

▲ grasslands

▲ rainforest

▲ coral reef

▲ orangutan

▲ camel

▲ shark

▲ mountain goat

▲ zebra

B. Complete the sentences. Use the habitats and animals in exercise **A**.

1. Many countries near the equator have ____________. They contain hundreds of different plants and animals.
2. ____________ can live without water for many days. They are perfectly adapted to live in ____________.
3. The Great Barrier Reef in Australia is the biggest ___________ in the world. It is the home of ____________ and many kinds of fish.
4. Kenya is famous for its ____________. Tourists come from all over the world to see the animals, like lions, elephants, and ____________.
5. The highest ___________ in the world are in Nepal. Not many animals live there. If you are lucky, you may see a ____________.

Grammar: Real conditionals

Result clause (future tense)	*If* clause (simple present tense)
The climate **will** change	if we **continue** to burn fossil fuels.
We **will** lose many valuable animals	if we **destroy** their habitats.

*Real conditionals can be written with the result clause first.
*These conditionals do not need a comma.

A. Match the result clauses to the correct *if* clauses.

1. Our coral reefs will die ___
2. We will lose many useful plants ___
3. You can rest tomorrow ___
4. It will reduce pollution ___
5. It's starting to rain. You'll get wet ___

a. if you finish your work today.
b. if more people use public transport.
c. if you don't leave now.
d. if ocean temperatures rise.
e. if we cut down all the trees.

B. Use these cues to write conditional sentences

1. children / suffer / if / don't take care of / animal habitats
   Our children will suffer if we don't take care of animal habitats.
2. fish / die / if / coral reef / die
   ____
3. visitors / not come / if / no / animals
   ____
4. live longer / if / exercise more
   ____
5. go / beach / if / no / rain
   ____

Conversation

Track 2-29

A. Listen to the conversation. What is John worried about? How can he help?

John: I'm very worried about all we hear and read about habitat destruction. It's important, but how can *I* help?
Sharon: You go to work by car. Right?
John: Yes.
Sharon: It will help if you go to work by bus.
John: How will that help?
Sharon: Buses carry lots of passengers, that means you use less gasoline per person. Less pollution, less climate change, less habitat destruction. Right?
John: Yes, and I save money as well.
Sharon: Right!

B. Practice the conversation with a partner. Switch roles and practice it again.

Real Language

You can say *Right* (rising tone) at the end of a statement to check information. You can also use *Right* (falling tone) to show you agree.

Goal 3 **Talk about how our actions can have positive consequences**

Work with a partner. Choose an important problem or environmental issue. Make a list of the things you can do to help. Tell your partner what positive consequences your actions will have.

◀ Hawaiian monk seal

◀ Illinois chorus frog

Reading

A. Discuss these questions with a partner.

1. These animals are in danger of extinction. Where do they live? In what kind of habitat?
2. Why is it important to look after animal habitats?

B. Answer the questions.

1. Why is the number of fish going down? ______________________________
2. If we stop fishing, what will happen? ______________________________
3. Why is it important to look after wetlands? ______________________________
4. Which are we losing more quickly, coral reefs or wetlands? ______________
5. Why are coral reefs dying? __________ ______________________________

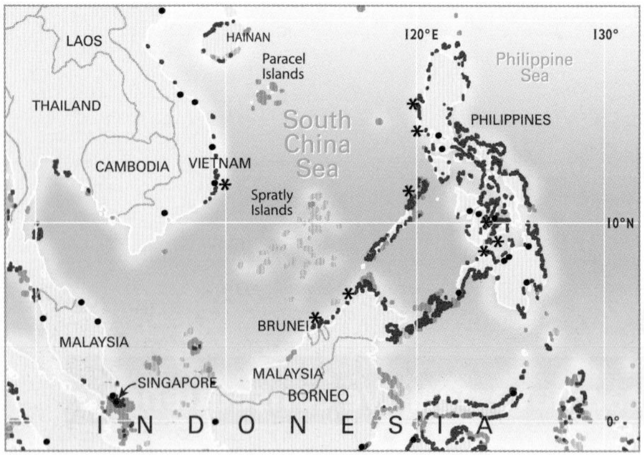

▲ endangered coral reefs

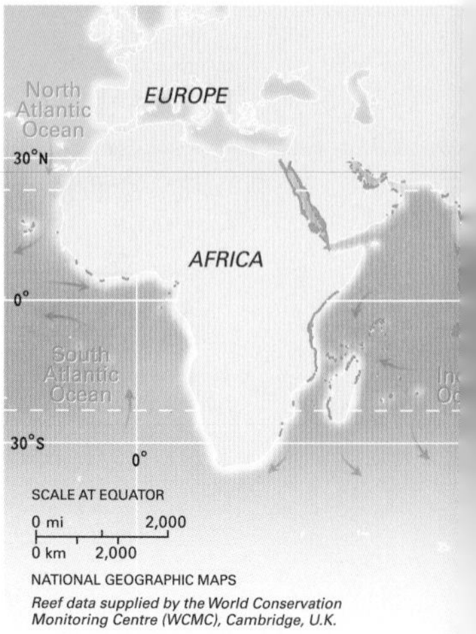

Habitat Destruction

OCEANS

Fish are like money in the bank. If you overspend, soon you will have no money. If we overfish, soon we will have no more fish. Fishermen now have bigger boats than in the past and they can catch more fish, so the number of fish is going down. Many scientists want to reduce or stop fishing completely in many parts of our oceans so the number of fish can **recover**.

WETLANDS

Freshwater and saltwater wetlands remove pollutants and provide habitat for fish, birds, and other animals. Many people, especially in Southeast Asia, depend on wetlands for food.

One hundred thirty-two nations have signed the Convention on Wetlands. However, the results have been **disappointing**. From the Amazon Basin to Iraq, we are **draining** wetlands for agriculture, dams, and development. Scientists estimate that we have lost 50 percent of our wetlands in the last 100 years. If we continue, there will be no wetlands left in 100 years.

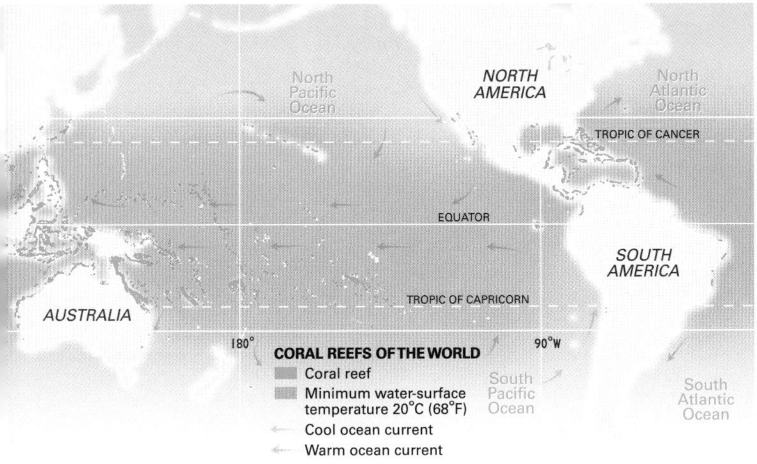

▲ coral reefs of the world

CORAL REEFS

A quarter of all animals that live in the sea live in coral reefs. They are the rainforests of the sea. However, we have lost 27 percent of our coral reefs in the past 50 years according to the Coral Reef Alliance. Why are they dying? Man—sometimes directly, sometimes indirectly—is the problem. Fishermen use **explosives** and **poison** to kill fish. They kill the fish but they also kill the coral. Ocean temperatures have increased due to climate change. Coral needs water to be at exactly the right temperature. If the water is too hot, the coral will die. So man's activities are indirectly killing the coral reefs.

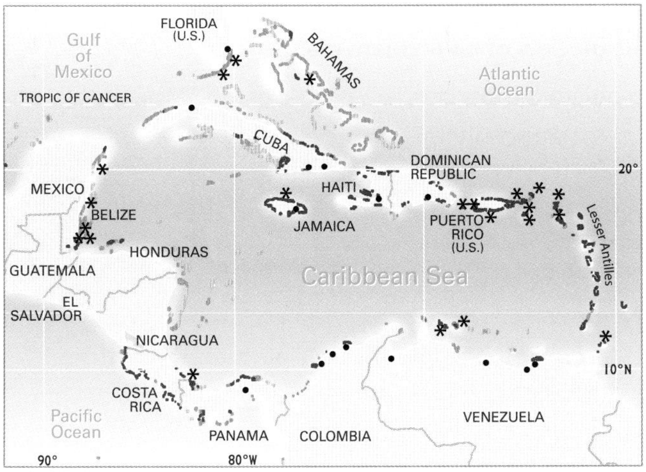

▲ endangered coral reefs

Word Focus

recover = to get back the same amount
drain = to remove water
disappointing = When something is *disappointing* it is not what you wanted or expected.
explosive = like a bomb
poison = a chemical that kills living things

Writing

Complete the letter to a magazine editor. Use the information you have learned in the article and your own ideas.

Dear Editor,

I read your article with interest and I agree with all you say. But what can the individual do?

The answer to the overfishing problem is simple. If everyone stops eating fish, ______________

____

The problem of the wetlands is more complicated because it is political. If people write to their senators, ______________

____

____

The loss of coral reefs is partly caused by climate change, so if ______________

______________________, that will help.

But how can **one** person change everything, I hear you say. Well, if **everyone** does something,

____

Yours sincerely,

Earl B. Butler
Wisconsin

Goal 4 Discuss ways to prevent habitat destruction

Work with a partner. Talk about the things you will do to prevent habitat destruction.

E VIDEO JOURNAL *THE MISSING SNOWS OF KILIMANJARO*

Before You Watch

A. Label the pictures with words from the box.

melt	**glacier**	**deforestation**

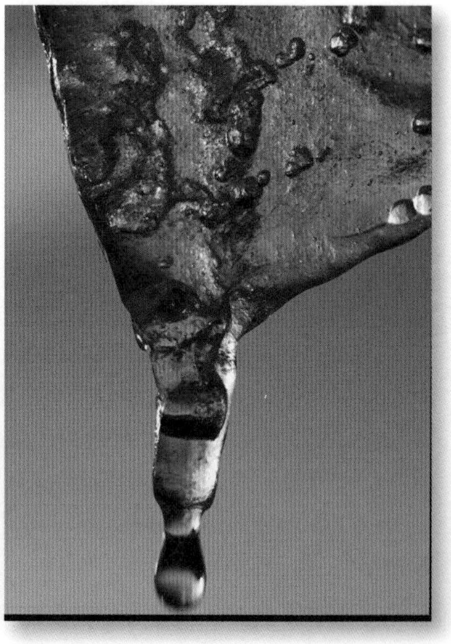

__________ __________ __________

B. Read the chain of actions and consequences. Number the sentences to make a similar chain.

Cars and airplanes produce carbon dioxide. > Carbon dioxide makes the atmosphere hotter. > The glaciers of Kilimanjaro melt.

___ The glaciers of Kilimanjaro get smaller.
___ There is less water in the atmosphere.
_1_ People cut down trees.
___ There is less rain and snow.

While You Watch

A. Watch the video. Fill in the numbers and dates.

1. Kilimanjaro is nearly __________ miles high.
2. It is around __________ miles south of the equator.
3. Ernest Hemingway published "The Snows of Kilimanjaro" in __________.
4. The glaciers on Kilimanjaro are __________ years old.
5. Experts now predict that the mountain's glaciers could completely disappear by the year __________.

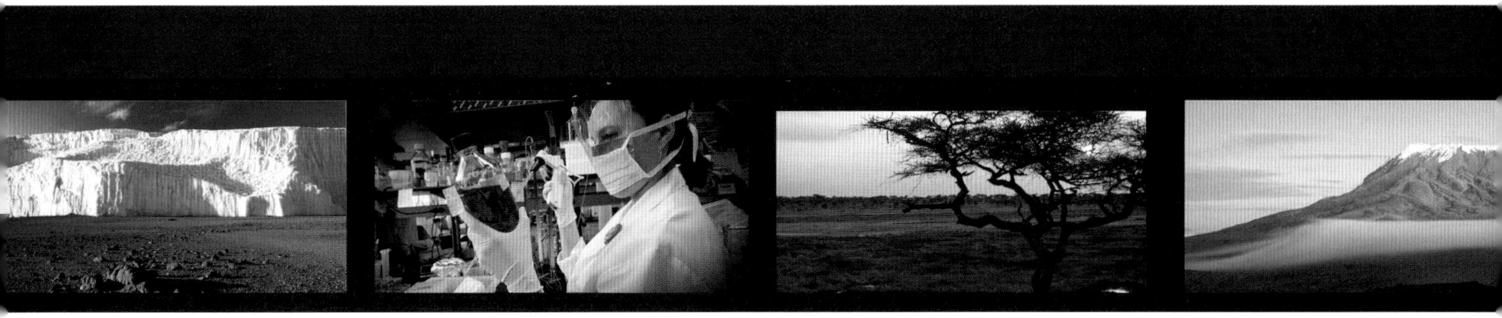

B. Answer the questions.

1. Why are the glaciers of Kilimanjaro important for the people who live near the mountain? ______________________
2. Why are the glaciers of Kilimanjaro important for Tanzania? ______________________
3. Why are the glaciers disappearing? ______________________

After You Watch

Discuss this question with a partner. Is there anything that *you* can do to stop the melting of Kilimanjaro's glaciers?

Communication

Choose a photo. Describe it to your partner.
Discuss the different causes of the changes you see.

STUDENT A

▲ the Rhone Glacier in Switzerland, 1849

STUDENT B

▲ the Rhone Glacier today

Activity 1

Look at the picture. Discuss the questions.

a. Where is Carmen from?
b. How old is she?
c. Can you read her writing?
d. Are there any mistakes?
e. Is she worried?
f. Do you make mistakes with your English?
g. Are mistakes important?

Activity 2

Work with a partner.

STUDENT A

Describe Keiko's clothes to a partner.

STUDENT B

Describe Ayame's clothes to a partner.

▲ Ayame Tanaka and her daughter Keiko.

Discuss these questions together.

a. Do you think Ayame likes Keiko's clothes? How do you know?
b. Do you think young people should wear traditional clothes? Give your reasons.

Activity 3

Work with a partner.

▲ Francine Patterson and Koko

STUDENT A

Describe the picture to a partner. What is Koko doing? What expression does he have on his face? What are Francine's feelings?

▲ Jane Goodall and chimpanzees

STUDENT B

Describe the picture to a partner. What are Jane and the chimpanzees doing? Describe their feelings.

Discuss together.
Which picture do you prefer? Why?

Activity 4

Work with a partner.

STUDENT A

Describe the photo to a partner. How many children are there? Where are they from? What are they doing? Where are they? Are they bored?

STUDENT B

Describe the photo to your partner. Where are the people? What are they doing? What are they wearing? What are their feelings?

Discuss these questions

a. Do people in your country like to read?
b. Do you prefer to read a book or go to the movies?

Activity 5

Work with a partner. Make a list of all the objects in the picture you can name in five minutes. Read your list to the class.

Activity 6

A. Work with a partner. Choose a person from one of the pictures. Describe him or her to your partner. What does the person look like? What is he or she doing? What are his or her feelings? Guess their nationality.

B. Look at the people. Discuss these questions with a partner. What is their relationship? Are they friends, brother and sister, husband and wife? Are they happy together? What happened before the photo was taken?

SKILLS INDEX

Test-taking skills

Topics

Video Journal

Vocabulary

Writing

CREDITS

TEXT

22–23 Adapted from "The Wild Mix of Trinidad and Tobago," by A.R. Williams: National Geographic Magazine, March 1994, **22–23** Adapted from "Brazil: Moment of Promise and Pain," by Priit J. Vesilind: National Geographic Magazine, March 1987, **22–23** Adapted from "Upbeat, Downbeat, Offbeat New Orleans: The Many Faces of MardiGras," by Priit J. Vesilind: National Geographic Magazine, January 1995, Steve Raymer/National Geographic Image Collection; **54** Adapted form "Jenny Daltry, Herpetologist, Emerging Explorer," National Geographic News Public Website, **58–59** Adapted from "Scaling the Dragon's Spires of Ha Long Bay, Vietnam," by Lynn Hill: National Geographic Magazine, December 1997, **70–71** "In the Wonderland of Peru," by Hiram Bingham: National Geographic Magazine, April 1913, **82–83** Adapted from "The Secret Language Dolphins," by Crispin Boyer: National Geographic Kids Magazine, June/July 2007, Issue 371, **94–95** Adapted from "Powering the Future," by Michael Parfit: National Geographic Magazine, August 2005, **106–107** Adapted from "Silk: The Queen of Textiles," by Nina Hyde: National Geographic Magazine, November 2005, **118–119** Adapted from "New Wrinkles on Aging," by Dan Buettner: National Geographic Magazine, October 1999, **130–131** Adapted from "Unveiling the Universe" by Kathy Sawyer: National Geographic Magazine, October 1999, **142–143** Adapted from "State of the Planet" by Michael Kelsius: National Geographic Magazine, September 2002.

ILLUSTRATION

iv-v: National Geographic Maps; **4:** National Geographic Maps; **5, 7, 8:** Nesbitt Graphics, Inc.; **10, 11, 12:** National Geographic Maps (all); **17, 19:** Nesbitt Graphics, Inc.; **22:** National Geographic Maps; **24:** National Geographic Maps; **32:** (t to b) photos.com, Nesbitt Graphics, Inc., Scott Espie/istockphoto, Hu Xiao Fang/ Shutterstock; **36:** National Geographic Maps; **40:** Keith Neely/illustrationOnLine.com; **41, 42, 44:** Nesbitt Graphics, Inc.; **48:** National Geographic Maps; **49, 53:** Nesbitt Graphics, Inc.; **58:** Phil Howe/illustrationOnLine.com; **59:** (l) National Geographic Maps, (r) Nesbitt Graphics, Inc.; **60:** National Geographic Maps; **67:** Nesbitt Graphics, Inc.; **68:** (l to r) Ralph Voltz/illustrationOnLine. com, Keith Neely/illustrationOnLine.com, Ralph Voltz/ illustrationOnLine.com (2), Keith Neely/ illustrationOnLine.com; **69:** Ralph Voltz/ illustrationOnLine.com; **70:** Phil Howe/ illustrationOnLine.com; **72:** National Geographic Maps; **80:** Nesbitt Graphics, Inc. (all); **84:** (l) National Geographic Maps, (r) shutterstock (all); **85: 92, 94:** Nesbitt Graphics, Inc. (all); **100:** Ted Hammond/illustrationOnLine. com (all); **103:** Nesbitt Graphics, Inc.; **108:** National Geographic Maps; **118:** (l) Nesbitt Graphics, Inc., (r) National Geographic Maps; **119:** National Geographic Maps.; **121, 125, 127, 136:** Nesbitt Graphics, Inc. (all); **139, 142, 143, 144:** National Geographic Maps (all).

PHOTO

iv: (t) Press Association via AP Images, (ml) Steve Raymer/National Geographic Image Collection, (mr) Richard Olsenius/National Geographic Image Collection, (b) Ralph Lee Hopkins/National Geographic Image Collection; **v:** (tl) Jodi Cobb/National Geographic Image Collection, (tr) Paul Chesley/National Geographic Image Collection, (b) Mark C. Ross/ National Geographic Image Collection; **2–3:** (l to r) Creatas/AGE Fotostock, Atlantide Phototravel/Corbis, Raul Touzon/National Geographic Image Collection, Tim Pannell/ Corbis; **4:** (1) Erwinova/Dreamstime, (2) Jack Fletcher/National Geographic Image Collection, (3) Robert Sisson/National Geographic Image Collection, (4) Christian Ziegler/National Geographic Image Collection, (5) Ed Kashi/ National Geographic Image Collection, (6) Winfield Parks/National Geographic Image Collection, (7) W. Robert Moore/National Geographic Image Collection, (8) Jason Edwards/National Geographic Image Collection; **5:** Mironov/istockphoto; **6:** (t to b) Peter Close/istockphoto, Simon Jarratt/Corbis, D Barton/Shutterstock, Andreblais/Dreamstime; **7:** Alaska Stock Images/National Geographic Image Collection; **8:** (top, l to r) Nicole S. Young/ istockphoto, photos.com, Carmen Martínez Banús/istockphoto, Monkey Business Images/ Shutterstock, (bottom, l to r) H-Gall/istockphoto, Louis Michaud/Shutterstock, Rhienna Cutler/ istockphoto, David Freund/istockphoto; **9:** Peter Close/Dreamstime; **10:** (t) Ivars Silis/National Geographic Image Collection, (b) Kevin Fleming/National Geographic Image Collection; **11:** (tl) Joel Sartore/National Geographic Image Collection, (tr) 4774344sean/Dreamstime, (m) William Albert Allard/National Geographic Image Collection, (b) Robert Essel NYC/Corbis; **12–13:** (l to r) Jung Yeon-Je/AFP/Getty Images (2), Stanislav Komogorov/Shutterstock, David White/Alamy, Andre Seale/Peter Arnold, photos. com, Stanislav Komogorov/Shutterstock, Jung Yeon-Je/AFP/Getty Images; **12:** (m) H. Edward Kim/National Geographic Image Collection, (b) Atlantide Phototravel/Corbis; **13:** (m) Dennis Sabo/Shutterstock, (b) H. Edward Kim/National Geographic Image Collection; **14–15:** (l to r) Rich Iwasaki/age fotostock, C Hughes/ Dreamstime, Nikonart/Dreamstime, Monkey Business Images/Dreamstime; **16:** (1) Monkey Business Images/Dreamstime, (2) Rmarmion/ Dreamstime, (3) Orange Line Media/ Shutterstock, (4) PhotostoGo.com, (5) Ivan Polushkin/Dreamstime, (6) Monkey Business Images/Dreamstime, (7) photos. com, (8) Paul Kim/Shutterstock, (9) Monkey Business Images/ Dreamstime, (10) PhotostoGo.com, (11) Duard Van Der Westhuizen/Dreamstime, (12) Joshua Blake/istockphoto; **18:** Imageshop/SuperStock; **19:** Paul Kim/Shutterstock; **20:** (tl) photos.com, (tr) istockphoto, (bl) Sam Abell/National Geographic Image Collection, (br) Joanna B. Pinneo/National Geographic Image Collection; **22:** (tl) Dudley M. Brooks/National Geographic Image Collection, (ml) Stephanie Maze/National Geographic Image Collection, (br) Tyrone Turner/National Geographic Image Collection; **23:** Michael Nichols/National Geographic Image Collection; **24–25:** (l to r) Scott Leigh/ istockphoto, Steve Raymer/National Geographic Image Collection, Mike Brake/Shutterstock, Steve Raymer/National Geographic Image Collection, Mike Brake/Shutterstock, Eugenia Garcia-Valdecasas/Dreamstime, Steve Raymer/ National Geographic Image Collection, Scott Leigh/istockphoto; **24:** (ml) Syracuse Newspapers/L. Long/The Image Works, (mr) Shutterstock, (bl) Bruce C. Murray/Shutterstock, (br) K. & H. Benser/zefa/Corbis; **25:** (m) Ted Spiegel/National Geographic Image Collection, (b) Antonio Jorge Nunes/Shutterstock; **26–27:** (l to r) Franz Pfluegl/Dreamstime, Oote Boe Photography/Alamy, James Steidl/Shutterstock, Hugo Maes/Shutterstock; **28:** (top, l to r) Eliza Snow/istockphoto, PhotostoGo.com, Digital Vision/Getty Images, James Steidl/Shutterstock,

Stockbyte/Getty Images, (bottom, l to r) Galyna Andrushko/Shutterstock, photos.com, Bruno Domingos/Reuters/Corbis, Timur Kulgarin/Shutterstock; **29:** Steve Reed/Shutterstock; **30:** (t) Jacom Stephens/istockphoto, (m) Justin Sullivan/Getty Images, (b) Jon Feingersh/zefa/Corbis; **31:** (left, t to b) Oote Boe Photography/Alamy, photos.com, James Steidl/Shutterstock, PhotostoGo.com, (right, t to b) Galyna Andrushko/Shutterstock, Justin Sullivan/Getty Images, Bruno Domingos/Reuters/Corbis, Stockbyte/Getty Images, Digital Vision/Getty Images; **32:** (tl) Elena Kalistratova/Shutterstock, (tr) Oleksiy Maksymenko/Alamy, (bl) Elwood Chu/Shutterstock, (br) Tom Young/istockphoto; **34:** Stockbyte/Getty Images; **35:** (l) Max Rossi/Reuters/Corbis, (r) Aleksander Bochenek/istockphoto; **36–37:** (l to r) Richard Olsenius/National Geographic Image Collection (2), Karen Kasmauski/National Geographic Image Collection, Richard Olsenius/National Geographic Image Collection, Joseph H. Bailey/National Geographic Image Collection, Brandon Baker/Alamy, Richard Olsenius/National Geographic Image Collection (2); **36:** (ml) Boris Djuranovic/Shutterstock, (mr) vera bogaerts/Shutterstock, (bl) Jan Tyler/istockphoto, (br) Lisa F. Young/Shutterstock; **37:** (b) Richard Olsenius/National Geographic Image Collection; **38–39:** (l to r) K Ovregaard/Cole Grou/age fotostock, Ahmet Ihsan Ariturk/Dreamstime, David Sanger photography/Alamy, David Coleman/Alamy; **41:** (tl) bramalia/Shutterstock, (tr) Laurent Renault/Shutterstock, (bl) Martin Firus/istockphoto; **42:** Catherine Karnow/National Geographic Image Collection; **43:** (t) Igor Burchenkov/Dreamstime, (b) Lucian Coman/Dreamstime; **44:** (top, l to r) Shutterstock (all), (bottom, l to r) istockphoto, Elena Schweitzer/Shutterstock, dyoma/Shutterstock, Graca Victoria/Shutterstock; **45:** Brad Killer/istockphoto; **46:** (l) Ben Russell/istockphoto, (r) Alasdair Thomson/istockphoto; **47:** (tl) Yury Zaporozhcheko/Dreamstime, (bl) Zheng Bin/Dreamstime, (bm & br) istockphoto; **48–49:** (l to r) Paul Chesley/National Geographic Image Collection, Joe Scherschel/National Geographic Image Collection, Paul Chesley/National Geographic Image Collection, photos.com, Joe Scherschel/National Geographic Image Collection (3), Paul Chesley/National Geographic Image Collection; **48:** (middle, l to r) Keith Flood/istockphoto, photos.com, Achim Prill/istockphoto, Peter Heiss/istockphoto, Brian J. Skerry/National Geographic Image Collection; **49:** (middle, t to b) Gallo Images/Alamy, Joe Scherschel/National Geographic Image Collection, istockphoto, (mr) photos.com, (br) Pawel Strykowski/Dreamstime, Rhouck/Dreamstime; **50–51:** (l to r) robcocquyt/Shutterstock, Antonio Ros/Dreamstime, xc/Shutterstock, Buzz Pictures/SuperStock; **52:** (tl) Suprijono Suharjoto/Dreamstime, (1) Tomasz Tulik/Dreamstime, (2) Pete Saloutos/Shutterstock, (3) Andreas Gradin/Shutterstock, (4) Gordon Wiltsie/National Geographic Image Collection, (5) Andres Rodriguez/Dreamstime, (6) Phase4Photography/Shutterstock, (7) Nicholas Rjabow/Dreamstime; **53:** JHDT Stock Images LLC/Shutterstock; **54:** (top, l to r) Bull's-Eye Arts/Shutterstock, Corbis/JupiterImages, Diego Cervo/Shutterstock, (bottom, l to r) Orange Line Media/Shutterstock, Nicholas Moore/istockphoto, Eric Renard/istockphoto; **56:** (tl) Mayskyphoto/Shutterstock, (tr) Tony Tremblay/istockphoto, (bl) Sean Nel/Dreamstime, (br) nikolpetr/Shutterstock; **57:** Kzenon/Shutterstock; **58:** (t) Henrik Trygg/Corbis, (b) Peter Gudella/Shutterstock; **59:** Christoph Papsch/Peter Arnold; **60–61:** (l to r) Carl De Souza/AFP/Getty Images, Peter Macdiarmid/Getty Images, Press Association via AP Images, istockphoto, Press Association via AP Images, PA/TopFoto/The Image Works, Kheng Guan Toh/Shutterstock, Press Association via AP Images; **60:** (ml) Ng Han Guan/AP Images, (mr) Jose Gil/Shutterstock, (bl) Tom Uhlman/AP Images, (br) Carl De Souza/AFP/Getty Images; **61:** (m) Peter Macdiarmid/Getty Images, (b) istockphoto; **62–63:** (l to r) Alison Wright/National Geographic Image Collection, age fotostock/SuperStock, Richard Nowitz/National Geographic Image Collection, David Evans/National Geographic Image Collection; **64:** (tl) Monkey Business Images/Dreamstime, (1) Konstantin Sutyagin/Shutterstock, (2) Adam Borkowski/Dreamstime, (3) J. D. Heaton/age fotostock, (4) istockphoto, (5) PhotostoGo.com, (6) istockphoto, (7) Max Alexander/Getty Images; **65:** Michael J. Doolittle/The Image Works; **66:** istockphoto; **67:** (t) Medford Taylor/National Geographic Image Collection, (middle, l to r) Robert Sisson/National Geographic Image Collection, Specta/Shutterstock, Dan Westergren/National Geographic Image Collection, ratluk/Shutterstock, (m) photos.com, (bottom, l to r) istockphoto, gary yim/Shutterstock, nfsphoto/Shutterstock, James Harrison/istockphoto; **70–71:** Hiram Bingham/National Geographic Image Collection (all); **72–73:** (l to r) Thomas Barrat/Shutterstock, Ralph Lee Hopkins/National Geographic Image Collection, Gina Martin/National Geographic Image Collection, Joel Shawn/Shutterstock, Ralph Lee Hopkins/National Geographic Image Collection, Gina Martin/National Geographic Image Collection, Joel Shawn/Shutterstock, Ralph Lee Hopkins/National Geographic Image Collection; **72:** (m) Celso Pupo/Shutterstock, (b) Ersler Dmitry/Shutterstock; **73:** (m) Thomas Barrat/Shutterstock; **74–75:** (l to r) The Art Archive/Musée du Louvre Paris, Pipa100/Dreamstime, Photononstop/SuperStock, Corbis RF/Photolibrary; **76:** (1) photos. com, (2, 3) istockphoto, (4 to 6) photos.com, (7) forest badger/Shutterstock, (8) Mischa/Shutterstock; **78:** Stepanov/Shutterstock; **79:** (t) Chris Schmidt/istockphoto, (b) photos.com; **80:** (top, l to r) istockphoto (2), HomeStudio/Shutterstock, Monkey Business Images/Shutterstock, (bottom, l to r) Edyta Pawlowska/Shutterstock, photos.com, Martinmark/Dreamstime, istockphoto; **81:** istockphoto; **82:** (tl) Albert Gea/Reuters/Corbis, (br) Flip Nicklin/Minden Pictures/National Geographic Image Collection; **83:** Franco Banfi/Peter Arnold; **84–85:** (l to r) Michael and Patricia Fogden/Minden Pictures/National Geographic Image Collection, Roy Toft/National Geographic Image Collection, Chris Johns/National Geographic Image Collection, Michael Nichols/National Geographic Image Collection, Tim Fitzharris/Minden Pictures/National Geographic Image Collection, Gerald Hinde/Getty Images, Chris Johns/National Geographic Image Collection, Tim Fitzharris/Minden Pictures/National Geographic Image Collection; **85:** (m) Roy Toft/National Geographic Image Collection; **86–87:** (l to r) istockphoto, Photowitch/Dreamstime, Jodi Cobb/National Geographic Stock, PhotoDisc/SuperStock; **88:** (top, l to r) istockphoto (all), (bottom, l to r) Andres Rodriguez/Dreamstime, Chris Rose/Getty Images, Thomas M Perkins/Shutterstock, istockphoto; **89:** David Young Wolff/PhotoEdit; **90:** Niderlander/Dreamstime; **91:** (t) istockphoto, (b) Digital Vision/Getty Images; **92:** (t to b) istockphoto (2), Nikolay Postnikov/Shutterstock, Despot/Shutterstock, Margojh/

Dreamstime, PhotoPips/Shutterstock, Salima/Shutterstock, istockphoto; **93:** Izaokas Sapiro/Dreamstime; **94, 95:** Sarah Leen/National Geographic Image Collection; **96–97:** (l to r) Gina Sanders/Shutterstock, Lucian Coman/Shutterstock, Christopher Pillitz/Getty Images, Lynsey Addario/Corbis, Falk Kienas/Shutterstock, John Stanmeyer/National Geographic Image Collection, Lucian Coman/Shutterstock, Lynsey Addario/Corbis; **96:** (middle, l to r) Kateryna Potrokhova/Shutterstock, Alex Kuzovlev/Shutterstock, istockphoto, Steve and Donna O'Meara/National Geographic Image Collection, Medford Taylor/National Geographic Image Collection; **97:** (m) Falk Kienas/Shutterstock; **98–99:** (l to r) PhotostoGo.com, A. Ramey/PhotoEdit, Justin Guariglia/National Geographic Image Collection, Monkey Business Images/Dreamstime; **101:** Natalie Shmeliova/Dreamstime; **102:** Bill Aron/PhotoEdit; **103:** (tl) Aflo/Corbis, (tr) STOCK4B GmbH/Alamy, (bl) PhotostoGo.com, (br) Fancy/Veer/Corbis; **104:** (top, l to r) istockphoto (2), Tiziana and Gianni Baldizzone/Corbis, image100/Corbis, istockphoto, photos.com; **106:** Cary Wolinsky/National Geographic Image Collection, Les Cunliffe/Dreamstime; **107:** (tl) Luis Marden/National Geographic Image Collection, (tr) Cary Wolinsky/National Geographic Image Collection, (bl) istockphoto, (br) J. Baylor Roberts/National Geographic Image Collection; **108–109:** (l to r) Jodi Cobb/National Geographic Image Collection, Lee Prince/Shutterstock, istockphoto, Luis Marden/National Geographic Image Collection, istockphoto (2) Luis Marden/National Geographic Image Collection, Lee Prince/Shutterstock; **108:** istockphoto; **109:** (m) July Flower/Shutterstock, (b) istockphoto; **110–111:** (l to r) Randy Faris/Corbis, PhotostoGo.com, Jeff Greenberg/Peter Arnold, Zhang Bo/istockphoto; **112:** (tl) Jamie Grill/Getty Images, (bl) Tony Wear/Shutterstock, (middle, l to r) Daphne Buter/Dreamstime, istockphoto, PhotostoGo.com, Kurhan/Dreamstime, (bottom, l to r) Studiovespa/Dreamstime, Pavel Siamionau/Dreamstime, Maximilian Stock Ltd/PhotoCuisine/Corbis, istockphoto; **113:** Creatista/Shutterstock; **114:** (l) istockphoto, (m) Martina Ebel/Shutterstock, (r) Inc/Shutterstock; **115:** (tl) Radius Images/Photolibrary, (tr) istockphoto, (mr) Blend Images/Getty Images, (bl) Gregor Kervina/Shutterstock, (br) Sharon Dominick/istockphoto; **116:** (t) Ellen B. Senisi/The Image Works, (b) istockphoto; **117:** PhotostoGo.com; **118:** Olgalis/Dreamstime; **119:** David Mclain/National Geographic Image Collection; **120:** (ml) Joel Sartore/National Geographic Image Collection, (mr) Mark C. Ross/National Geographic Image Collection, (bl) Lorraine Swanson/Shutterstock, (br) John Burcham/National Geographic Image Collection; **120–121:** (l to r) image100/Corbis, istockphoto (3), Suzanne Tucker/Shutterstock, Dex Images/Corbis, istockphoto (2); **122–123:** (l to r) Annie Griffiths Belt/National Geographic Image Collection, NASA/National Geographic Image Collection, Mandy Godbehear/Shutterstock, Jerry Lampen/Reuters/Corbis; **124:** (1) Monkey Business Images/Shutterstock, (2) katja kodba/Shutterstock, (3) Starblue/Dreamstime, (4) Anne Kitzman/Shutterstock, (5 to 7) istockphoto, (8) David Young-Wolff/PhotoEdit; **126:** (tl) istockphoto, Andre Blais/Shutterstock, Andres Rodriguez/Dreamstime, Shutterstock; **128:** (1) Andresr/Shutterstock, (2) Mandy Godbehear/Shutterstock, (3) Rolf Bruderer/Jupiterimages, (4) koh sze kiat/Shutterstock, (5) photos.com, (6) Chunche/Dreamstime.com, (7) istockphoto, (8) Hongqi Zhang/Dreamstime; **129:** istockphoto; **130:** (tl) ESA and NASA/National Geographic Image Collection; (tr) Joe McNally/Getty Images; **132–133:** (l to r) ESA and NASA/National Geographic Image Collection, NASA (7); **132:** (middle, l to r) NASA/National Geographic Image Collection (2), NASA; **133:** (m) ESA and NASA/National Geographic Image Collection, (b) Peter Ginter/National Geographic Image Collection; **134–135:** (l to r) PhotostoGo.com, Ron Giling/Peter Arnold, Bob Daemmrich/PhotoEdit, Haider Yousuf/Dreamstime; **136:** (l) Schaefer Elvira/Shutterstock, (r) David Young-Wolff/PhotoEdit; **137:** photos.com; **138:** (l) Image Source/JupiterImages, (m) O. Louis Mazzatenta/National Geographic Image Collection, (r) Nicole Duplaix/National Geographic Image Collection; **140:** (top, l to r) Carsten Peter/National Geographic Image Collection, Michael Melford/National Geographic Image Collection, Tui De Roy/Minden Pictures/National Geographic Image Collection, Michael and Patricia Fogden/Minden Pictures/National Geographic Image Collection, Chris Newbert/Minden Pictures/National Geographic Image Collection, (bottom, l to r) Konrad Wothe/Minden Pictures/National Geographic Image Collection, Richard Nowitz/National Geographic Image Collection, Norbert Wu/Minden Pictures/National Geographic Image Collection, Michael S. Quinton/National Geographic Image Collection, Gerry Ellis/Minden Pictures/National Geographic Image Collection; **142:** (t1) Bill Curtsinger/National Geographic Image Collection, (t2) Suzanne L. & Joseph T. Collins/Photo Researchers, (m) Alaska Stock Images/National Geographic Image Collection, (b) Tim Fitzharris/Minden Pictures/National Geographic Image Collection; **144–145:** (l to r) Ralph Lee Hopkins/National Geographic Image Collection, Mark C. Ross/National Geographic Image Collection, David Pluth/National Geographic Image Collection, Kondrachov Vladimir/Shutterstock, David Pluth/National Geographic Image Collection, emin kuliyev/Shutterstock, Ralph Lee Hopkins/National Geographic Image Collection, David Pluth /National Geographic Image Collection; **144:** (middle, l to r) Gerry Ellis/Minden Pictures/National Geographic Image Collection, istockphoto, Paul Nicklen/National Geographic Image Collection; **145:** (bl) Science Museum/SSPL, (br) James Balog/National Geographic Image Collection; **146:** (t) Cary Wolinsky/National Geographic Image Collection, (b) Getty Images/Jupiterimages; **147:** (t) Gorilla Foundation/AP Images, (b) Michael Nichols/National Geographic Stock; **148:** (t) Cary Wolinsky/National Geographic Image Collection, (b) Ed Bock/Corbis; **149:** (t) René Milot/National Geographic Image Collection, (bl) Robert Madden/National Geographic Image Collection, (br) G P Bowater/Alamy.